Japan's Finance and Taxation, 1940-1956

JAPAN'S FINANCE AND TAXATION

1940-1956

By SABURO SHIOMI

TRANSLATED BY

SHOTARO HASEGAWA

1957 COLUMBIA UNIVERSITY PRESS *New York*

Published in Great Britain, Canada, India, and Pakistan
by the Oxford University Press
London, Toronto, Bombay, and Karachi

Library of Congress Catalog Card Number: 57-10937

Manufactured in the United States of America

Foreword

THE problem of taxation is of major concern to any modern country in the world today, and is being studied with especially keen attention in many countries. The characteristic of the postwar tax system of Japan is that it has been considerably democratized under American influence. The culmination was reached by the recommendation of the Shoup Mission, headed by Dr. Carl S. Shoup, by which the fundamental principle for taxation was established and the framework was completed. There remain, however, manifold problems to be solved, such as adjustments to various financial, economic, and social policies, and particularly to long-established national mores. A thorough re-examination of the system is necessary.

Dr. Saburo Shiomi's present work offers not only technical explanations of past developments and the present status of the Japanese taxation system, but also competent analytical studies of the system in close connection with economic realities. It further gives valuable suggestions in many respects as to what a future taxation system should be.

As a professor at Kyoto University for many years, Dr. Shiomi has conducted researches in the science of public finance, with particular reference to the taxation system and related problems. At present, he is the president of the Japan Tax Association, a member of the Local Administrative System Investigation Commission and several other commissions, and is taking an active part in the study of tax problems. He is no doubt a foremost authority on the science of public finance and taxation in Japan.

I hope that this book is read widely in other countries. It will be fortunate indeed if it serves to stimulate the interest of people abroad in the Japanese taxation system so as to invite their instructive advice and suggestions.

HISATO ICHIMADA
Minister of Finance of Japan
Former Governor of the Bank of Japan

November, 1956
Tokyo, Japan

Preface

IN this volume, Dr. Saburo Shiomi fills an important gap in the Western World's knowledge of Japanese taxation by integrating the war and pre-war developments in the Japanese tax system with the sweeping changes of the post-war period. All who have occasion to study the finances of Japan are correspondingly in his debt. Students of income taxation, in particular, will find much of interest here. While differences of opinion are to be expected on the goals to be sought and the means to be employed in tax policy, Dr. Shiomi's fair-minded approach, his scholarship, and his refusal to be drawn into doctrinaire positions all combine to make the book required reading for anyone who wishes to understand something of the enormous problems that Japan has faced, and met, in reconstructing a tax system shattered by war, while at the same time she was called upon to finance a complex modern economy.

CARL S. SHOUP
Professor of Economics

Columbia University
April, 1957

Author's Preface

NO nation in contemporary history ever faced so dramatic a destiny as did Japan during the last fifteen years. Whatever she had assiduously accumulated since the beginning of the Meiji Era, a period of nearly eighty years, was completely reduced to ashes by the waste of four years of war. Unconditional surrender on August 15, 1945, was followed by a seven-year period of occupation by the Allied Forces, then the independence for which the people longed was reinstated in 1952. The cold reality, however, is that eighty million people are crowded together on four small islands, and that hundreds of difficult and complicated problems confront them on the hard road to rehabilitation.

Whatever criticisms may have been or may now be directed against the policies of the Allies during the occupation, the fact remains that the people today enjoy a fairly stabilized life. Their hopes for a happy and prosperous future are chiefly due to the appropriate policies of the Allied Forces, particularly those of the United States. Japan should appreciate her good fortune because, under the impact of political developments soon after the war, the situation could have been much worse.

There is no denying that some of the many experimental measures taken by the Allied Forces in the fields of economics, politics, and sociology were either too drastic or too novel for the traditionally conservative people of Japan; but the democratization of the nation, the fundamental principle which underlay every measure, has profoundly influenced the minds of the Japanese. It is hoped that it will make healthy progress and gradually be integrated into their very lives.

The United States of America has poured millions of dollars into Japan for this purpose, and naturally the American people have a right to know how these monies have been spent and what has been accomplished by them. This book, of course, does not claim to explain everything. The author will be satisfied if it throws a sidelight on the occupation policies in regard to finance, particularly the taxation system, and also if it serves to warn peoples of other lands how easily modern war can destroy a nation's finance and throw a whole people into misery and confusion.

The author has been a professor at Kyoto University for the past thirty-five years and is now professor emeritus. He has not only been a student of finance, particularly of taxation from the academic point of view, but has been in direct contact with actual problems through the posts he has held; as a councillor for the taxation system of the Finance Ministry and for the Bank of Japan, as President of the Japan Tax Association, as Chairman of the Tax Administration Council, and as vice-chairman of the Tax System Research Council. The extraordinary happenings in finance and taxation during the period which the author has witnessed and experienced have given rise to valuable records and data, and his scholastic conscience does not permit him to leave them to be consigned to oblivion. An attempt, therefore, has been made to compile all data collected by him in the pursuit of his study in the past.

The task of translation into English has been principally the charge of Shotaro Hasegawa, co-author, a personal friend of the author. He has spent many years abroad, working at various branch offices of the former Mitsui & Co., Ltd., Tokyo, a well-known international mercantile house. He is at present with the Osaka Gas Company, Ltd., as an adviser.

The author has been fortunate in receiving assistance from many persons. Thanks are due to the Ministry of Finance, the Autonomy Agency, various local bodies, the Japan Tax Association, and particularly to the Bank of Japan, which generously assigned staff-members Mr. R. Yonemoto and Mr. H. Tomana to his aid. Thanks are also due to Mr. E. Ozaki, a coordinator of the Economic Planning Board, and to Mr. S. Chigira, former president of the Mitsubishi Bank, now a member of the Policy Board of the Bank of Japan, who has graciously offered his valuable support to the author's work. A special indebtedness is acknowledged to Dr. Carl S. Shoup of Columbia University, through whose kind assistance the publication of this book was made possible. None of these individuals or organizations are responsible, however, for the conclusions reached in the present volume.

To summarize the contents, Part One treats of the changes in the economic life of the people that provide the background of Japan's finance and taxation system and also deals with problems of inflation.

Part Two explains the tax system drawn up by Japan in 1940, just one year before World War II, and describes the changes that took place during the war. The early occupation policy, which was either too experimental or too drastic, was hardly contributive to the recovery of the country, and the fiscal measures taken by the Japanese government, such as the capital levy system and new currency system, were also found useless against the march of inflation. The later occupation policies, however, were more constructive; they were directed toward the control of inflation. The preparation of a "super-balanced" budget formulated by Mr. Joseph Dodge and the establishment of a new tax system recommended by Dr. Carl S. Shoup were the culminating measures which effectively tided the nation over the critical situation.

Part Three recounts the history of the establishment and development of the income tax and the corporation tax in Japan. It shows how hard the Japanese have tried to modernize and improve their tax system since the first income tax law was promulgated in 1877, and how modest and open-minded their attitude has been in adopting the best tax systems of advanced countries.

Part Four contains two areas of special research. Ever since World War I, it has been an academic topic whether war would widen or narrow the discrepancy between rich and poor. In the case of Japan we present statistical evidence that although this discrepancy was widened in World War I, the exact reverse was true of World War II. The second area of research concerns the problems of local finance, as illustrated by the city of Osaka, the author's birthplace. He shows how the economic and social life of the city together with sixty-seven neighboring cities, towns, and villages were changed by World War II.

SABURO SHIOMI

Kyoto University
August, 1957

Contents

List of Tables

List of Charts

PART ONE

Background, 1940-1956

I. *Drastic Changes in Japan's Economy*

DURING the twelve years from 1940 to 1951, Japan experienced a series of the most tragic events in her history. She recklessly rushed into World War II, which ended in inevitable defeat and which was followed by unprecedented economic chaos and social unrest. It was only toward the end of the period that signs of recovery appeared. Meanwhile, reforms had been effected in public finance as well as in the taxation system. The tax reforms introduced in the first half of the period were intended to rationalize the system and to augment the treasury revenues to meet the colossal sums needed for the prosecution of the war. The purpose of the later reforms was twofold: an adjustment of public finance to counter the inflation manifest at the war's end, and the financial and economic democratization essential to the building of a new, democratic nation.

In the period under study, Japan's economy experienced drastic changes. The writer attempts to survey these changes with particular reference to the amount of currency in circulation, the level of production, and the price level, as shown by various economic indices. Records of note issues of the Bank of Japan and those of deposits and loans of city banks will throw light on the first phase of the study, that of currency and circulation. For production, the production index for manufacturing and mining and the composite index of industrial activity and production prepared by the Economic Scientific Section (ESS) of General Headquarters (GHQ), Supreme Commander of Allied Powers (SCAP) are referred to. In studying price movements, we have made use of the wholesale price index in Tokyo, computed by the Bank of Japan. To facilitate comparisons, the indices of the five-year average for 1932–36 (a period that may be considered as normal) are taken as a basis figure of 100. Table 1 shows how abnormally the Japanese economy moved during the period, 1940–1956.

Following the Manchurian and China struggles, the weight of production was placed on heavy industry, as required by the semi-wartime national structure. All the energy of the country, political as well as

TABLE 1

ECONOMIC INDICATORS, 1940–1956

(Volume in million yen)

Year	BANK OF JAPAN: Bank-note Issue: Volume	BANK OF JAPAN: Bank-note Issue: Index	ALL BANKS (EXCEPT BANK OF JAPAN): Deposits: Volume	ALL BANKS (EXCEPT BANK OF JAPAN): Deposits: Index	ALL BANKS (EXCEPT BANK OF JAPAN): Loans: Volume	ALL BANKS (EXCEPT BANK OF JAPAN): Loans: Index	*Wholesale Price Index in Tokyo*	*Production Index for Manufacturing and Mining*	*Composite Index of Industrial Activity and Production*
1932–36 average	1,646	100.0	12,273	100.0	9,258	100.0	100.0	100.0	100.0
1940	4,777	290.2	31,189	253.1	18,371	198.4	171.6	165.5	163.0
1941	5,978	363.2	37,801	308.0	20,985	226.7	183.9	171.5	170.0
1942	7,148	434.3	46,569	379.4	24,856	268.5	200.0	164.6	164.1
1943	10,266	623.7	56,328	459.0	32,354	349.5	214.0	195.5	190.5
1944	17,745	1,078.1	77,926	634.9	51,154	552.5	242.5	219.1	208.8
1945	55,440	3,368.2	119,829	976.4	97,621	1,054.5	366.3	86.4	87.1
1946	93,397	5,674.2	144,869	1,180.4	146,406	1,581.4	1,701.6	33.1	48.6
1947	219,141	13,313.5	234,376	1,909.7	168,243	1,817.3	5,035.8	40.2	57.1
1948	355,280	21,584.4	505,349	4,117.6	381,348	4,119.1	13,378.6	58.1	74.1
1949	355,311	21,586.3	792,018	6,453.3	679,052	7,334.8	21,832.7	77.2	93.5
1950	422,063	25,641.7	1,048,564	8,543.7	994,746	10,744.7	25,811.2	97.3	112.7
1951	506,385	30,764.6	1,506,308	12,273.3	1,517,813	16,394.6	35,755.4	136.4	147.4
1952	576,431	35,020.1	2,223,820	18,119.6	2,128,022	22,985.0	36,536.0	146.8	158.4
1953	629,891	38,267.0	2,707,612	22,061.0	2,671,286	28,853.0	38,510.0	185.0	199.3
1954	622,061	37,792.2	3,036,687	24,742.7	2,911,968	31,453.5	38,258.0	197.3	212.5
1955	673,890	40,941.1	3,724,382	30,348.6	3,195,818	34,519.5	37,567.3	213.6	230.0
1956	784,861	47,682.9	4,764,263	38,694.0	4,064,494	43,902.2	39,211.2	259.0	278.8

Note: Figures for the bank-note issues and deposits and loans of city banks represent the year-end balances. Indices of price and of industrial activity and production are annual average. With the exception of the industrial activity and production index (prepared by ESS, GHQ), all indices have been obtained through adjustment of figures furnished by the Statistics Department of the Bank of Japan.

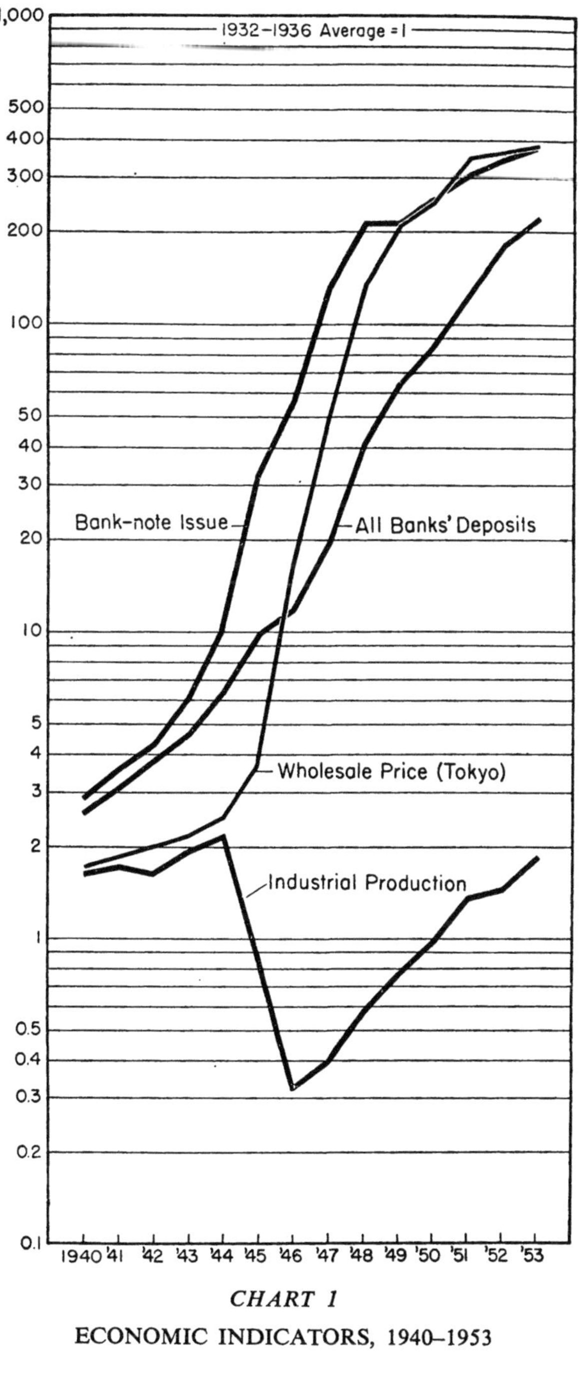

CHART 1

ECONOMIC INDICATORS, 1940–1953

economic, was concentrated on increasing production. As a result, industrial activity and production in 1940 rose to 163.0 from the 1932–36 average, as seen in Table 1. These efforts were further spurred after the country went into World War II, and the index ascended to a peak of 208.8 in 1944 through industrial reorganization and coordination. However, the expansion in production was for military consumption only, not for an increase in capital goods that would have made possible a higher level of production in later periods, and unless some of the increase in national money income could be absorbed, inflation would be bound to follow.

History shows that taxation has always been considered the most reliable source of revenue for war costs, but Japan, anticipating a short war, relied chiefly on national bond issues for this purpose. The bond issues were absorbed mainly by financial institutions. At the same time consumption of goods was restricted, in order to restrain the use of purchasing power by the public, and prices and wages were placed under control to maintain commodity prices at certain levels. Consequently, between 1940 and 1944 the price index rose only moderately, from 171.6 to 242.5, whereas that of currency in circulation advanced sharply from 290.2 to 1,078.1. However, these counterinflation measures eventually lost their effectiveness and, from 1943 on, the war bonds issued surpassed the absorbing capacity of private financial institutions and began to accumulate in the Bank of Japan. On the other hand, despite the vigorous government policy of pushing production, a shortage of raw materials began to be felt by the metal industry in 1944, and was followed by a decline in the pivotal machinery industry by 1945. This critical situation was aggravated by frequent enemy air-raids over the mainland; production was seriously disrupted, and even before the war ended, Japan had lost her ability to continue it.

As the war came to a close, the frenzied pace of war productivity halted, but the mental vacuum created by defeat caused an even greater paralysis of national production. Though no accurate figures are available to illustrate the conditions just before and after the termination of the war, indices compiled by the National Economic Society record the decline of production as given below. The figures enable one to discern the amazing speed with which Japan's productive power was virtually destroyed.

Toward the close of the war and immediately after, huge amounts of war expenditures were disbursed. Under the hypnotic influence of a

PRODUCTION INDICES
(1931–33 = 100)

		Mining	*Iron and Steel*	*Textiles*	*Electricity and Gas*
1944		152.5	161.1	22.2	197.4
1945	April	126.8	82.5	9.5	134.2
	June	120.6	60.3	10.7	121.5
	August	56.0	9.5	4.5	74.6
	October	23.5	5.2	4.5	77.5
	December	33.0	7.9	5.1	97.8

patriotic spirit for total war, the government measures, however hard and uncomfortable for people, had been well observed. Strict controls over commodity prices had also been fairly well maintained, but once authority collapsed, resentment that had long been held back was suddenly released, and black marketeers operated openly, thus allowing the prices of all commodities to soar. The people, already suffering from a dearth of the bare necessities of life, rushed to convert their holdings of money into goods. There was a surge of applications for bank loans and withdrawals of deposits. The index of bank loans went up from 552.5 in 1944 to 1,054.5 in 1945, whereas that of deposits showed a much smaller rise, from 634.9 to 976.4. It is to be added that time deposits, the most stable of all, markedly decreased, thereby altering the structure of bank deposits.

To meet the crisis and to curb inflation, deposits were frozen, currency was converted into new yen notes, and the price structure was revised. All these measures failed to restore the production level, and the destruction of the circulation order prohibited price and wage controls. Inflation mounted steadily. The price index rose from 242.5 in 1944, to 366.3 in 1945, to 1,701.6 in 1946. If black-market quotations were included, it could easily be imagined how much higher the figures would be. The currency index advanced from 1,078.1 in 1944, to 3,368.2 in 1945, to 5,674.2 in 1946.

The situation was not improved in 1947. The additional supply of government and private credits was used to garner inflation profits; it was not put into production recovery, and therefore led to the draining of domestic stocks. Official prices were revised again and again without avail. In 1948, however, the priority production system in operation since the preceding year began to show its effects, and the production indices of the mining and metal industries rose from 56.4 and 16.1 respectively, in 1946, to 90.1 and 48.7 in 1948. With the improvement in these key industries, the composite indices of industrial activity and production also advanced to 74.1. Not only that, official price revisions could now be made much closer to black-market quotations as well as to authorized market prices, and a vigorous national campaign to promote savings proved fruitful, once the public fear of another currency reform was removed. Nevertheless, inflation was still rampant, under the stimulus of funds released in 1948 by treasury and banking sources in an attempt to promote production.

In 1949, the principle of "stabilization rather than rehabilitation" was established in accordance with the so-called "Dodge Line," and a super-balanced budget was drawn up to check further currency issues. In order to counter the deflationary trend resulting from this treasury policy, financial institutions created credits to the extent that the rate of bank-loan increase over deposit increase continued to stay relatively too high. As a result of the Dodge policy, however, currency was so successfully stabilized that the amount of currency remained almost unchanged during 1948 and 1949. In addition, thanks to the disinflationary policy, the production index rose to 93.5 in 1949. Though financial retrenchment took the course of abolishing various government subsidies, necessitating price revisions, confidence in money was restored, and living was stabilized as inflation terminated. It was unfortunate, indeed, for Japanese economy that the Korean war broke out in June, 1950, before the basis of stability was firmly laid. On the other hand, production was stimulated above the prewar level to meet increasing overseas demands.

The war altered the production structure from top to bottom. As we have seen, the industrial setup moved from light to heavy industry as demanded by the war, and this transformation has not yet been readjusted. For example, on the basis of a prewar 100, production in the metal industry was 223.5 in the peak year of 1943 and 718.0 in the machine industry in 1944, whereas the textile industry (predominant from the Taisho Era, that is, from 1912) fell as low as 13.7 in 1944. Of the manufacturing industries, durable goods registered 432.2 and nondurable goods 47.8 in 1944. These indices stood at 100.7 and 53.4, respectively, in 1949 and 121.5 and 75.5 in 1950. The figures show that the postwar economic effort, as planned by the priority production system, was primarily concentrated on rehabilitation, even though somewhat at the expense of national consumption.

The loss of territory and of population is the most significant of all the great changes that occurred in Japan's economy during the period. The effect on the population of the loss of territory is made clear by comparing the national census of October 1, 1939, with that of October 1, 1950.

TABLE 2

AREA, POPULATION, AND POPULATION DENSITY BEFORE AND AFTER WORLD WAR II

	Pre-Surrender Territory	*Post-Surrender Territory*	
	(as in 1939)	*(as in 1939)*	*(as in 1950)*
Area (in 1,000 sq. km.)	678	383	383
Population (in units of 1,000)	103,247	73,114	83,772
Density of population (per 1 sq. km.)	152	191	219

In making the comparison, Japan's territory as of 1950 is for the present assumed as that exclusive of her former colonial territories and undecided regions: the Kuriles, South Karafuto, the Bonin Islands, Korea, the Ryukyus, Formosa, the Pescadores, Kwantung province (Manchuria) and the South Pacific islands. On this basis, Japan's territory as of 1950 has been reduced to 56 percent of its extent in 1939. In contrast, a comparatively small drop (19 percent) was shown in population; in consequence, the density of population rose from 152 to 219. A comparison of the density of population in 1939 and in 1950 on the basis of area figures for the post-surrender territory also shows an increase, from 191 to 219. It must also be noted that the lost area represents a big loss in "quality," since these territories were producing centers of rice, sugar, soy beans, and salt. Without them, Japan is no longer self-sustaining but must import food. The intensified density of population plus the difficulty in obtaining necessary food is affecting every area of Japanese life. It is, therefore, of primary importance to take these vital factors—overpopulation and lack of resources—into proper consideration in arriving at a correct judgment on Japan's finance and taxation system.

TRENDS IN NATIONAL AND LOCAL FINANCE

Japan's national finance during the last fifteen years moved against a background of violent fluctuations. In any country wartime finance is invariably complex and is often difficult for an outsider to comprehend. The case of Japan is no exception. This is particularly true because here the national and local finances have been so closely interdependent that it has always been difficult to define their exact relationship. The national treasury has had numerous Special Accounts besides its General Account Proper (there were forty-nine Special Accounts in the fiscal year 1942); some Special Accounts are completely independent of the General Account, while others are dependent on it in varying degrees. A study of the trend of national and local finance must, therefore, take cognizance of these intricate relationships.

The elemental way to study the relations between national and local finance is to compare the General Account of national finance with those accounts other than Enterprise Accounts of local finance. The figures given in Table 3 have been prepared for the purpose.

TABLE 3

NATIONAL AND LOCAL EXPENDITURES (SETTLED ACCOUNTS), 1940–1955

(In million yen)

	National Finance		*Local Finance*		
	General Account (A)	*Index*	*Accounts Other than Those of Enterprises (B)*	*Index*	*B ÷ A*
1932–36 average	2,171	100.0	2,324	100.0	107.0
1940	5,860	269.9	2,848	122.5	48.6
1941	8,133	374.6	3,149	135.5	38.7
1942	8,276	381.2	3,484	149.9	42.1
1943	12,551	578.1	4,422	190.3	35.2
1944	19,871	915.3	3,864	166.3	19.4
1945	21,496	990.1	5,014	215.8	23.3
1946	115,207	5,306.6	27,780	1,195.4	24.1
1947	205,841	9,481.4	93,476	4,021.8	45.4
1948	461,974	21,279.3	259,070	11,147.6	56.1
1949	699,448	32,217.8	391,492	16,845.6	56.0
1950	633,295	29,170.1	522,563	22,485.5	82.5
1951	749,838	34,538.8	668,673	28,772.5	89.2
1952	873,942	40,255.3	842,045	36,232.5	96.3
1953	1,027,251	47,316.9	914,933	39,368.9	89.1
1954	999,588	46,042.7	967,722	41,640.3	96.8
1955	991,458	45,668.2	993,019	42,728.8	100.2

From the average figures for 1932-36, it can be assumed that, in a normal prewar fiscal year, the local expenditure was 107 percent of the national expenditure. On the outbreak of World War II, the national expenditure began to mount until in 1940 the situation was reversed,

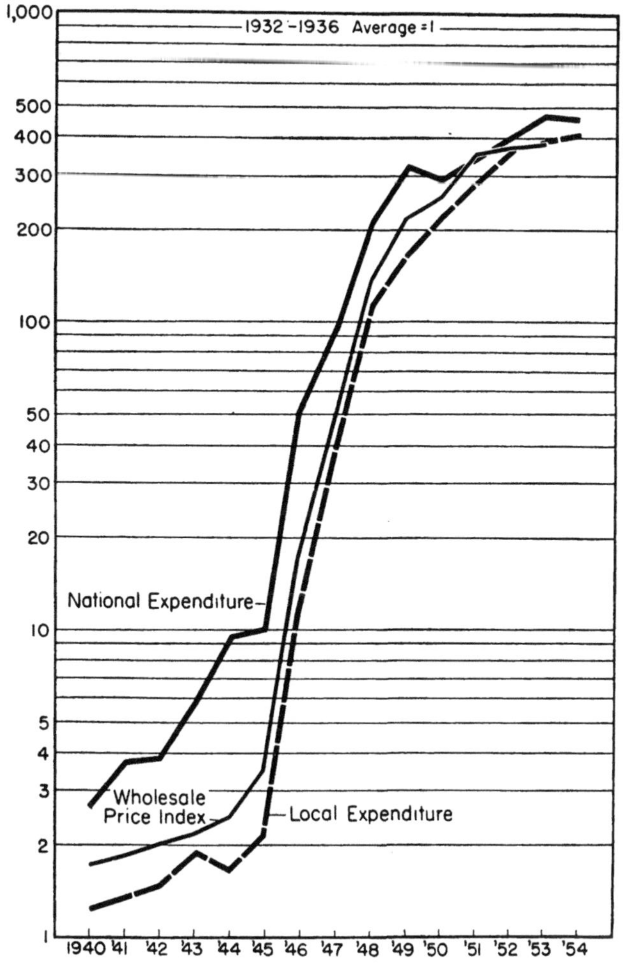

CHART 2

INDEX OF NATIONAL AND LOCAL EXPENDITURES COMPARED WITH PRICE INDEX, 1940–1954

and local expenditure dwindled to 48.6 percent of national expenditure; in 1944, it fell to a mere 19.4 percent. Since the end of the war, a gradual balance has been achieved and in 1954 the local expenditure rose to 98 percent of the national expenditure. Table 3 also shows that in 1955 national expenditure increased by 456 times over the prewar average, whereas local expenditure increased by 427 times.

The foregoing gives a general idea of the trend of national and local public finance. In proceeding a step further, some complicated overlapping accounts are soon discovered, such as the treasury's disbursements to prefectures, cities, towns, and villages; disbursements from prefectures to cities, towns, and villages; and also various contributions to the treasury from all these civic units. An attempt was made to eliminate these from the total of national and local expenditures. Moreover, in compiling Table 4, Enterprise Accounts have been omitted from local expenditures to balance the omission of non-war Special Accounts from national expenditures.

TABLE 4

CONSOLIDATED FIGURES OF NATIONAL AND LOCAL EXPENDITURES (SETTLED ACCOUNT), 1940–1955

(In million yen)

Fiscal Year	*National Expenditure*[a] *A*	*Local Expenditure*[b] *B*	*Total* *A + B*	*Duplications* *C*	*Net Expenditure* *A + B − C*	*Index*
1932–36 average	2,171	2,324	4,495	348	4,147	100.0
1940	10,982	2,848	13,830	813	13,017	313.9
1941	16,542	3,149	19,691	1,044	18,647	449.7
1942	24,406	3,484	27,890	1,244	26,646	642.5
1943	38,001	4,422	42,423	1,845	40,578	978.5
1944	86,159	3,864	90,023	1,602	88,421	2,132.2
1945	76,116	5,014	81,130	6,666	74,464	1,795.6
1946	115,207	27,780	142,987	17,885	125,102	3,016.7
1947	205,841	93,467	299,308	52,114	247,194	5,960.8
1948	461,974	259,070	721,044	139,633	581,411	14,020.0
1949	699,448	391,492	1,090,940	164,668	926,272	22,336.0
1950	633,295	522,563	1,155,858	238,934	916,923	22,110.6
1951	749,837	668,673	1,418,510	248,959	1,169,551	28,202.3
1952	873,942	842,075	1,716,017	308,075	1,407,914	33,950.1
1953	1,017,164	1,069,752	2,086,916	427,964	1,658,952	40,003.6
1954	999,458[c]	980,351	1,980,231	421,256	1,558,975	37,592.8
1955	991,458[c]	993,019	1,984,477	438,434	1,546,043	37,281.0

[a] 1932–36, 1946–55 = General Account. 1940–45 = Consolidated figures of the General Account and the Special Accounts for Extraordinary War Expenses.

[b] Accounts other than those of enterprise.

[c] Estimated figures.

Table 4 shows that the combined net volume of national and local expenditures gradually increased from 13,017 million yen in the fiscal year 1940, and after climbing to 926,272 million yen in 1949, slipped to 916,923 million yen in 1950, but jumped back to a high of 1,546,043 million yen in 1955. Compared with the 1932-36 average of 4,147 million yen, the 1955 volume represents a 372-fold increase.

The national expenditures cited in Table 4 represent only the General Account and the Special Account for extraordinary war expenses. Other Special Accounts are omitted from this table but must receive full consideration in a detailed analysis of the public finance of Japan, particularly the Special Account for Allotment of Local Allocation Tax and the Special Account of Receipts from capital levy. The total net national expenditure shown in Table 5 is obtained by removing only the overlapping parts of the General and Special Accounts from the combined total expenditure of both.

TABLE 5

NATIONAL EXPENDITURE: CONSOLIDATED FIGURES OF ESTIMATED EXPENDITURES OF GENERAL ACCOUNT AND SPECIAL ACCOUNTS, 1940–1954

(In million yen)

Fiscal Year	*Estimated Expenditures of General Account*	*Net Total Expenditures*	*Index*
1932–36 average	2,204	5,959	100
1940	6,173	16,988	285
1941	8,657	28,036	470
1942	9,317	35,044	588
1943	14,459	49,455	829
1944	21,838	95,614	1,604
1945	29,156	123,615	2,074
1946	119,087	192,253	3,226
1947	214,256	437,977	7,349
1948	414,462	1,065,503	17,878
1949	741,046	1,929,929	32,285
1950	664,576	1,992,136	33,425
1951	793,707	1,744,366	29,268
1952	932,535	1,787,273	29,993
1953	1,027,250	2,004,016	33,624
1954	999,588	2,056,664	34,508

Japan was completely disarmed and lost its overseas territories. This naturally reduced the number of Special Accounts, especially those relating to the War, Navy, and the Colonial Ministries, but others were rapidly created as circumstances demanded. The net amount of the average national expenditure for 1932-36, 5,959 million yen, rose 20-

TABLE 6

AMOUNT OF NATIONAL AND LOCAL BONDS, ISSUED, REDEEMED AND OUTSTANDING, 1940–1954

(In million yen)

	Total				*National Government Bonds*				*Local Government Bonds*			
Year	*Issued*	*Redeemed*	*Outstanding*		*Issued*	*Redeemed*	*Outstanding*		*Issued*	*Redeemed*	*Outstanding*	
1932–36 average	2,107	1,018	9,474	100.0	1,439	529	7,214	100.0	668	490	2,260	100.0
1940	7,024	197	30,027	316.9	6,754	0	27,008	374.4	270	197	3,019	133.6
1941	9,310	189	39,148	413.2	9,092	0	36,100	500.4	218	189	3,048	134.9
1942	14,452	189	53,411	563.8	14,155	0	50,255	696.6	297	189	3,156	139.6
1943	20,027	269	73,094	771.5	19,591	0	69,847	968.2	436	269	3,247	143.7
1944	27,673	1,219	99,548	1,050.7	27,550	949	96,448	1,337.0	123	270	3,100	137.2
1945	33,341	400	132,164	1,395.0	33,312	200	129,560	1,796.0	29	200	2,604	115.2
1946	21,405	470	153,099	1,616.0	21,258	323	150,495	2,086.2	147	147	2,604	115.2
1947	55,944	426	208,596	2,201.8	55,199	296	205,397	2,847.2	745	130	3,199	141.5
1948	38,785	2,762	244,620	2,582.0	37,856	2,409	240,845	3,338.6	929	353	3,775	167.0
1949	93,931	43,645	294,908	3,112.8	90,765	43,413	288,199	3,995.0	3,166	232	6,709	296.9
1950	28,682	50,774	271,394	2,864.6	28,420	47,231	269,387	3,734.1	262	3,543	2,007	88.8
1951	16,334	34,383	253,347	2,674.1	16,324	33,286	252,425	3,499.1	12	1,097	922	40.7
1952					60,502	10,266	302,657	4,195.4				
1953					204,009	44,661	462,005	6,404.2				
1954					22,379	11,751	472,633	6,551.6				

fold to 123,615 million yen in fiscal 1945, when the war ended, and 345 times to 2,056,664 million yen in 1951.

The first half of the period under review was the stage of "wartime finance"; at first the government relied both on taxes and on borrowing for revenue, but later, almost solely on borrowing, much of it from the Bank of Japan, inevitably stimulating inflation. Later efforts were made to halt the so-called public finance inflation. The "bonds-first" policy was replaced by the "taxes-first" policy. Measures were taken to reduce bond issues and to encourage bond retirement. The effect on the amount of outstanding issues is summarized in Table 6.

It will be noted that emphasis was placed on the issuing of bonds in the first half of the period and on the redemption of bonds in 1950 and 1951. Local government debt, in contrast, rose little during the war, but expanded in 1948 and 1949. The total amount of public bonds at

TABLE 7

VERTICAL AND HORIZONTAL RELATION BETWEEN NATIONAL AND LOCAL EXPENDITURES, 1951

(In million yen)

Expenditures	*Accounts*		
	A: General		B: Special
National	749,837		1,275,068
	A′: Other than enterprise		B′: Enterprise
Local	668,673		134,186
A + A′	1,418,510		
Duplications	248,959		
A + A′ − Duplications	1,169,551	Net amount of national and local expenditures	
A + B	2,024,905		
Duplications	423,460		
A + B − Duplications	1,601,445	Net amount of national expenditures	

the end of 1951 represented a 26-fold increase over the 1932-36 average. The rate of increase is comparatively small as compared with the 357-fold rise of commodity prices; it means that redemption of public bonds was actually brought about by inflation.

The data on government expenditure can be cross-tabulated, for any one year, by level of government and by type of account. Such a tabulation is presented in Table 7 for the year 1951, with duplications eliminated.

TABLE 8

COMPOSITION OF NATIONAL TAX REVENUES BY FISCAL YEARS, 1940–1951

(In thousand yen)

Fiscal Year	*General Account Revenue Total (A)*	*Taxes*	*Stamp Revenue*	*Profit of the Monopoly Bureau*	*Total of Ordinary Tax Revenues (B)*	*B ÷ A*	*Extraordinary Tax Revenues (Special Accounts of North China Incident Tax, Capital Levy, etc.)*	*Total of Tax Revenues (C)*	*Index*	*C ÷ A*
1932–36 average	2,251,088	853,087	78,175	192,496	1,123,757			1,123,757	100.0	49.9
1940	6,444,988	3,729,564	135,607	352,170	4,217,341	65.4	1,593	4,218,934	375.4	65.4
1941	8,601,695	4,369,896	145,699	414,930	4,930,525	57.3	809	4,931,334	438.8	57.3
1942	9,191,608	6,806,129	154,328	568,440	7,528,897	81.9	205	7,529,102	670.0	81.9
1943	14,009,735	8,639,887	203,595	1,116,585	9,960,067	71.1	15	9,960,082	886.3	71.1
1944	21,040,389	11,437,367	227,779	1,197,682	12,862,828	61.1	1	12,862,829	1,144.6	61.1
1945	23,487,487	10,337,172	162,167	1,056,193	11,555,532	49.2	....	11,555,532	1,028.3	49.2
1946	118,899,071	29,704,868	407,354	7,325,970	37,438,192	31.5	18,115,224	55,553,416	4,943.6	46.7
1947	214,467,253	146,525,718	936,252	42,139,145	189,601,115	92.7	18,287,046	207,888,161	18,499.4	96.9
1948	508,037,761	341,047,555	4,783,811	101,914,238	447,745,604	86.4	7,814,755	455,560,359	40,539.0	89.6
1949	758,611,762	509,169,742	8,980,711	118,232,000	636,382,453	83.9	2,469,000	638,851,453	56,849.6	84.2
1950	716,792,000	447,185,000	9,207,000	113,821,000	570,214,000	79.6	871,000	571,086,000	50,819.8	79.7
1951	895,483,000	593,508,000	10,524,000	118,331,107 [a]	722,363,107	80.6	414,304 [a]	722,777,411	64,317.9	80.7

[a] Estimated figures.

TRENDS IN NATIONAL AND LOCAL TAXES

National finance and local finance of Japan differ not only in the content of expenditures but also in the composition of revenues. Naturally, each has its own characteristic development.

In national wartime finance, revenue from government bonds occupied first place, though tax revenue was by no means ignored. Some time after the end of the war, emphasis was placed upon what was called a "super-balanced" budget, which adhered to the principle of taxes as the main source of revenue. The status of tax revenue in the General Account budget 1940-51 is shown in Table 8.

Here, "ordinary tax revenue" includes stamp revenues and profits of the Monopoly Bureau, and also such extraordinary taxes as Capital Levy. The percentage of taxes in the annual revenue of the General Account was lowest (46.7 percent) in fiscal 1946, and highest (96.9 percent) in fiscal 1947.

Local finance has, in addition to tax revenues proper, such non-tax revenues as national treasury disbursements, rents, and fees. Consequently, tax revenues are less important locally than nationally. The breakdown of local finance into tax revenue and non-tax revenues is shown in Table 9.

In Table 9, if we interpret "tax revenues" to include only "tax proper" and to exclude local apportionment taxes and local finance equalization grants, we find that the fiscal year 1946 witnessed the lowest proportion of these revenues (11.8 percent) and the fiscal year 1951 the highest (39.2 percent). It is characteristic of local finance that it relies on non-tax rather than tax revenues.

Table 10 illustrates the shifts of national and local taxes in the same period.

A review of total tax revenues on the basis of the 1932-36 average, discloses that they rose about threefold in fiscal 1940 and about sevenfold in fiscal 1945, the year of Japan's surrender. They rocketed to 453-fold in 1949 and 742-fold in 1955. Apparently influenced by wartime finance, the rate of expansion of national taxes has been greater than that of local taxes. The ratio between national and local taxes was 65:35 in 1932-36. This proportion was changed to 93:7 at the war's end, as a result of a marked increase in national taxes during the war. As public finance stabilized in succeeding years, the situation gradually

TABLE 9

COMPOSITION OF LOCAL REVENUES BY FISCAL YEARS, BY AMOUNT AND PERCENT OF ANNUAL TOTAL, 1942–1953
(In million yen)

			Tax Revenues								Non-Tax Revenues							
Fiscal Year	*Total Revenues (Other than Public Enterprises)*		*Tax Proper*		*Allotments of Local Apportionment*		*Total*		*National and Prefectural Disbursements*		*Public Bonds*		*Rent and Fees*		*Contributions*			
1932–36 average	2,851	100.0	596	20.9			2,255	79.1	330	11.9	925	32.4	292	10.2	44	1.5		
1942	4,825	100.0	933	19.3	608	12.6	3,284	68.1	764	15.9	495	10.3	404	8.4	120	2.5		
1943	6,050	100.0	991	16.4	670	11.1	4,389	72.5	1,242	20.5	582	9.6	565	9.4	97	1.6		
1944	4,235	100.0	862	20.4	684	16.2	2,689	63.4	897	21.2	513	12.1	467	11.0	81	1.9		
1945	5,361	100.0	985	18.4	848	15.8	3,528	65.8	1,517	28.3	411	7.7	517	9.7	109	2.0		
1946	31,705	100.0	3,725	11.8	2,586	8.2	25,394	80.0	15,423	48.6	3,226	10.2	1,844	5.8	710	2.2		
1947	100,020	100.0	20,198	20.2	19,362	19.3	60,460	60.5	32,350	32.3	14,327	14.3	2,320	2.3	3,594	3.5		
1948	277,500	100.0	77,709	28.0	49,883	18.0	149,908	54.0	88,778	32.0	23,905	8.6	6,684	2.4	7,018	2.5		
1949	414,694	100.0	142,440	34.2	67,731	16.4	204,523	49.4	113,117	27.3	27,347	6.6	12,289	3.0	7,089	1.7		
1950	544,949	100.0	188,280	34.5	108,450	19.9	248,219	45.6	126,634	23.2	32,825	6.0	15,163	2.8	7,772	1.4		
1951	693,656	100.0	272,263	39.2	120,004	17.3	301,389	43.5	138,940	20.0	53,299	7.7	19,477	2.8	10,833	1.6		
1952	853,089	100.0	307,765	36.1	145,000	17.0	400,324	46.9	174,961	20.5	70,756	8.3	25,600	3.0	15,495	1.8		
1953	1,072,900	100.0	336,200	31.3	137,900	12.9	598,800	55.8	310,400	28.9	106,800	10.0	32,200	3.0	17,600	1.6		

TABLE 10

NATIONAL AND LOCAL TAXES BY FISCAL YEARS, 1940–1955

Fiscal Year	Tax Revenues (In million yen)			Index			Comparative Index		
	National	*Local*	*Total*	*National*	*Local*	*Total*	*National*	*Local*	*Total*
1932–36 average	1,124	595	1,720	100.0	100.0	100.0	65.3	34.7	100.0
1940	4,219	984	5,203	375.4	165.4	302.5	81.1	18.9	100.0
1941	4,931	879	5,810	438.7	147.7	337.8	84.9	15.1	100.0
1942	7,529	934	8,463	669.8	157.0	492.0	89.0	11.0	100.0
1943	9,960	991	10,951	886.3	166.6	636.7	91.0	9.0	100.0
1944	12,863	862	13,725	1,144.4	144.9	798.0	93.7	6.3	100.0
1945	11,555	919	12,474	1,028.0	154.5	725.2	92.6	7.4	100.0
1946	37,438	3,726	41,164	3,330.8	626.2	2,393.3	90.9	9.1	100.0
1947	189,601	20,198	209,799	16,868.4	3,394.6	12,197.6	90.4	9.6	100.0
1948	447,746	77,709	525,455	39,835.1	13,060.3	30,549.7	85.2	14.8	100.0
1949	636,406	142,441	778,847	56,619.8	23,939.7	45,281.8	81.7	18.3	100.0
1950	570,849	188,281	759,130	50,787.3	31,643.9	44,135.5	75.2	24.8	100.0
1951	723,144	272,264	995,408	64,336.7	45,758.7	57,872.6	72.6	27.4	100.0
1952	843,004	307,773	1,150,777	75,000.4	51,726.6	66,905.6	73.3	26.7	100.0
1953	907,480	310,217	1,217,697	80,736.7	52,137.3	70,796.3	74.5	25.5	100.0
1954	906,283	349,252	1,255,535	80,630.2	58,697.8	72,996.2	72.2	27.8	100.0
1955	917,600	358,274	1,275,874	81,637.0	60,214.1	74,178.7	71.9	28.1	100.0

TABLE 11

NATIONAL TAXES: DIRECT, INDIRECT, AND OTHERS, 1940–1955

(In million yen)

Fiscal Year	Total Amount of National Tax			Direct Tax			Indirect Tax			Others		
	Amount	*Ratio of Increase*	*Percent*	*Amount*	*Ratio of Increase*	*Percent*	*Amount*	*Ratio of Increase*	*Percent*	*Amount*	*Ratio of Increase*	*Percent*
1932–36 average	1,124	100.0	100.0	373	100.0	33.2	655	100.0	58.3	96	100.0	8.5
1940	4,219	375.4	100.0	2,695	722.5	63.9	1,288	196.6	30.5	234	243.8	5.6
1941	4,931	438.7	100.0	3,163	848.0	64.1	1,516	231.5	30.7	251	261.5	5.2
1942	7,529	669.8	100.0	4,785	1,282.8	63.6	2,347	358.3	31.2	395	411.5	5.2
1943	9,960	886.1	100.0	5,627	1,508.6	56.5	3,859	589.2	38.7	473	492.7	4.8
1944	12,863	1,144.4	100.0	8,376	2,245.3	65.1	3,947	602.6	30.7	540	562.5	4.2
1945	11,555	1,028.0	100.0	7,334	1,966.2	63.5	3,514	536.5	30.4	707	736.5	6.1
1946	37,438	3,330.7	100.0	21,331	5,718.8	57.0	14,259	2,176.9	38.1	1,846	1,922.9	4.9
1947	189,601	16,868.4	100.0	99,409	26,651.2	52.4	82,571	12,606.3	43.5	7,621	7,938.5	4.1
1948	447,746	39,835.1	100.0	222,743	59,716.6	49.7	191,827	29,286.6	42.8	33,176	34,558.3	7.5
1949	636,406	56,619.8	100.0	344,374	92,325.5	54.1	243,783	37,218.8	38.3	48,249	50,259.4	7.6
1950	570,849	50,787.3	100.0	313,625	84,081.8	54.9	246,101	37,572.7	43.1	11,123	11,586.5	2.0
1951	723,144	64,336.7	100.0	424,986	113,937.3	58.8	285,784	43,631.1	39.5	12,372	12,887.5	1.7
1952	843,031	75,000.4	100.0	475,671	127,525.7	56.4	351,917	53,723.7	41.7	15,443	16,086.5	1.9
1953	942,521	83,854.2	100.0	507,308	136,007.5	53.8	412,458	62,970.7	43.8	22,755	23,703.1	2.4
1954	906,283	80,630.2	100.0	484,308	129,841.3	53.4	395,029	60,309.8	43.6	26,946	28,068.8	3.0
1955	917,600	81,637.0	100.0	473,106	126,868.1	51.6	419,198	63,999.7	45.7	25,296	26,350.0	2.7

returned to normal, the ratio in fiscal 1955 being 72 percent national taxes against 28 percent local taxes.

The relationship between direct and indirect national taxes is demonstrated in Table 11.

On the national level, the ratio between direct and indirect taxes was 33 percent to 58 percent in 1932-36. Distorted by the war, the ratio became 65 percent to 31 percent in 1944. It was 52 percent to 46 percent in 1955. Similar changes occurred on the local level. Table 12 compares the changes in the ratio of direct and indirect taxes on both levels in fiscal 1954. The direct and indirect taxes are itemized.

TABLE 12

DIRECT, INDIRECT, AND OTHER TAXES IN NATIONAL AND LOCAL FINANCES, 1954

(In million yen)

National Taxes			*Local Taxes*			*National and Local Taxes*	
	Amount	*Percent*		*Amount*	*Percent*	*Amount*	*Percent*
Direct			Direct				
Income	287,632		Enterprise	78,159			
Corporation	187,617		Inhabitants	87,796			
Accession	3,162		Municipal	92,404			
Revaluation	5,897		Others	18,409			
Total	484,308	53.4	Total	276,768	79.2	761,076	60.6
Indirect			Indirect				
Liquor	140,777		Tobacco	29,182			
Sugar	38,124		Amusement	16,941			
Gasoline	23,767		Electricity	17,570			
Commodity	24,398		Others	2,955			
Admissions	12,526						
Customs	25,000						
Monopoly bureau	130,437						
Total	395,029	43.6	Total	66,648	19.1	461,677	36.8
Others			Others				
Securities	1,014		Real estate	3,938			
Traveling	2,379		Others	1,898			
Bourse	345						
Tonnage	240						
Stamp	22,968						
Total	26,946	3.0	Total	5,836	1.7	32,782	2.6
Total	906,283	100.0	Total	349,252	100.0	1,255,535	100.0

In fiscal 1954, direct taxes constituted 53 percent of national taxes and 79 percent of local taxes, whereas indirect taxes constituted 44 percent of the national total and 19 percent of the local. It has been advocated that the ratio of direct tax revenues in both national and local

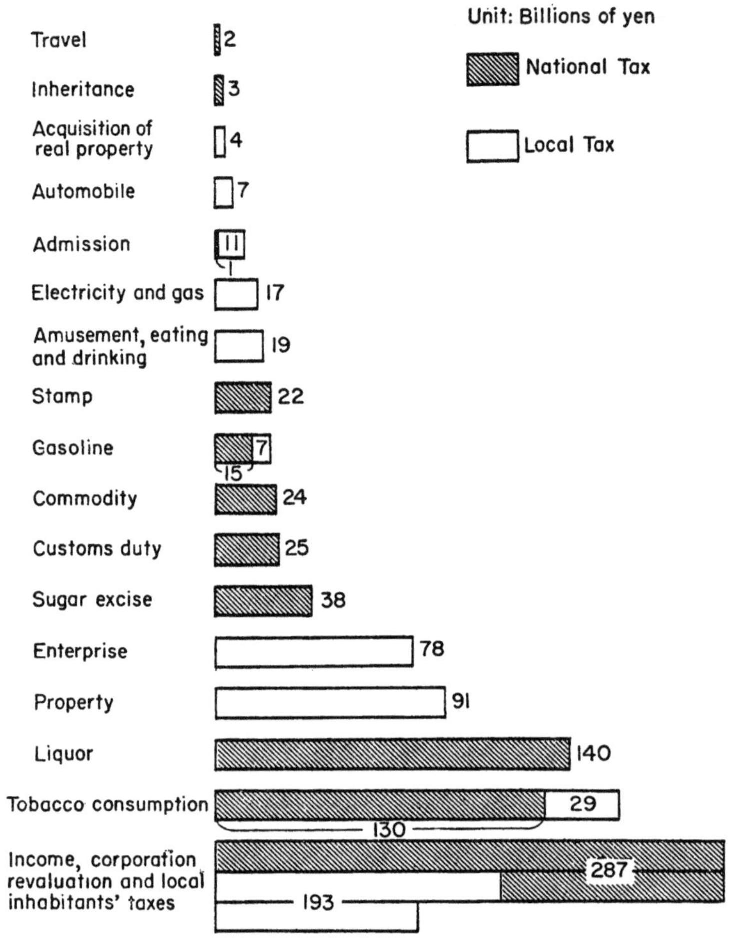

CHART 3

SOURCES OF TAX REVENUES IN JAPAN, 1954

finance be brought up to 75 percent of the total tax revenues. Others have suggested the need of greater attention to indirect taxes.

Table 13 summarizes the per capita tax burden. This is generally computed in relation to national income, but the necessary statistics for that computation are not available with the requisite degree of accuracy.

Therefore the tax burden is here presented simply in relation to population and is adjusted by the Tokyo wholesale price index.

Even if the population figure remains the same, its economic significance differs according to the varying number of adults and minors. Accordingly, the per capita tax figure is not necessarily a precise measure of the individual burden. The meaning of the figure also differs, as already stated, according to the varying amount of national income, even if both the total population and constituent ages remain the same.

TABLE 13

PER CAPITA TAX BURDEN, 1940–1954

Year	*Total Amount* (In million yen)	*Population* (By 1,000)	*Actual Per Capita Tax* (In yen)	*Per Capita Tax Adjusted by Tokyo Wholesale Price Index* (In yen)
1932–36 average	1,720	68,248	25	25
1940	5,203	73,114	71	41
1941	5,810	74,067	78	42
1942	8,463	75,114	113	57
1943	10,951	76,464	143	67
1944	13,725	73,064	188	78
1945	12,474	71,996	174	48
1946	41,164	72,875	565	33
1947	209,799	78,627	2,668	53
1948	525,455	80,217	6,550	49
1949	778,847	82,338	9,459	43
1950	759,130	83,200	9,124	35
1951	995,408	84,573	11,769	33
1952	1,150,777	85,852	13,404	37
1953	1,217,697	87,000	13,996	36
1954	1,255,535	88,081	14,254	37

Nevertheless, it is noteworthy that the amount of per capita tax burden, which was 25 yen in 1932-36, rose to 14,403 yen, roughly 576 times greater, in 1954. But the decline in purchasing power of currency should be considered in making such a comparison: an adjustment made on the basis of the Tokyo wholesale price index also indicates that the tax burden increased—from 25 yen in 1932-36 to 37 yen in 1954. Another consideration that cannot be overlooked in making a fair comparison is the substantial drop in national income brought on by the loss of territory and the devastation of production capacity that resulted from the war. Taking that factor into account, it is apparent that tax

TABLE 14

PAST AND PRESENT INCUMBENTS OF THE OFFICE OF FINANCE MINISTRY OR LOCAL FINANCE OFFICE, 1940–1955

	Ministry of Finance		*Ministry for Home Affair, Local Autonomy Agency, Local Finance Commission*		
Year	*Finance Minister*	*Director of Taxation Bureau*	*Home Minister, Minister of State*	*Director of Local Affair Bureau, Director of Executive Office*	*Governor of the Bank of Japan*
1940	Aoki (Jan.) Sakurauchi (July) Kawata	Ohya (Dec.) Matsukuma	Ohara (Jan.) Kodama (July) Yasui (Dec.) Hiranuma	Hazama (July) Tomeoka	Yuhki
1941	Kawata (July) Ogura (Oct.) Kaya	Matsukuma	Hiranuma (July) Tanabe (Oct.) Tohjoh	Tomeoka (Oct.) Narita	Yuhki
1942	Kaya	Matsukuma	Tohjoh (Feb.) Yuzawa	Narita (June) Furui	Yuhki
1943	Kaya	Matsukuma	Yuzawa (Apr.) Andoh	Furui (July) Arai	Yuhki
1944	Kaya (Feb.) Ishiwata	Matsukuma (March) Tanaka	Andoh (July) Ohtate	Arai (April) Nadao	Yuhki (March) Shibuzawa
1945	Ishiwata (Feb.) Tsushima (Apr.) Hirose (Aug.) Tsushima (Dec.) Shibuzawa	Tanaka (Feb.) Ikeda	Ohtate (April) Abe (Aug.) Yamazaki (Oct.) Horikiri	Nadao (April) Irie	Shibuzawa (Oct.) Araki

1946	Shibuzawa (May) Ishibashi	Ikeda	Horikiri (Jan.) Mitsuchi (May) Ohmura	Irie (Jan.) Kohri	Araki (June) Ichimada
1947	Ishibashi (May) Katayama (June) Yano (June) Kurusu	Ikeda (Feb.) Maeo (Dec.) Hirata	Ohmura (Jan.) Uehara (May) Kimura (Dec.)	Kohri (Feb.) Hayashi (Dec.)	Ichimada
1948	Kurusu (March) Kitamura (Oct.) Yoshida (Oct.) Izumiyama (Dec.) Ohya	Hirata	Nomizo (Oct.) Iwamoto	Ogita	Ichimada
1949	Ohya (Feb.) Ikeda	Hirata	Iwamoto (Feb.) Kimura	Ogita (Dec.) Suzuki	Ichimada
1950	Ikeda	Hirata	Kimura (Jan.) Honda (June) Okano	Suzuki (May) Ogita	Ichimada
1951	Ikeda	Hirata	Okano	Ogita	Ichimada
1952	Ikeda (Oct.) Mukai	Hirata (Dec.) Watanabe	Okano (Oct.) Honda	Ogita (July) Suzuki	Ichimada
1953	Mukai (May) Ogasawara	Watanabe	Honda (May) Tsukada	Suzuki	Ichimada
1954	Ogasawara (Dec.) Ichimada	Watanabe	Tsukada (Dec.) Nishida	Suzuki	Ichimada (Dec.) Araki
1955	Ichimada	Watanabe	Nishida (March) Kawashima (Nov.) Ohta	Suzuki	Araki
1956	Ichimada (Dec.) Ikeda	Watanabe (July) Hara	Ohta (Dec.) Tanaka	Suzuki	Araki (Nov.) Yamagiwa

burdens in Japan have become considerably heavier in the past fifteen years.

A review of the period beginning with the outbreak of World War II and ending with the conclusion of the Peace Treaty in San Francisco discloses that one of the major obstructions to stabilized finance has been the unsteady political situation in Japan. There have been twenty changes of Finance Minister, and twenty-three replacements of the Minister for Interior Affairs or State Affairs, the office responsible for local finance. Fortunately, the governor's office of the Bank of Japan, which regulates money and finance, has been spared frequent changes (there have been only four) and there have also been fewer replacements in the office of the chief of the Tax Bureau responsible for national taxation and the chief of the Local Tax Bureau in charge of local taxation, five in the former case and seven in the latter. This fact doubtless helped to prevent confusion in national and local finance, which was otherwise bound to occur.

It is creditable indeed that in these hectic times, both Mr. H. Ichimada, Governor of the Bank of Japan from June, 1946, until December, 1954, when he became the Finance Minister, and Mr. H. Ikeda, Finance Minister, 1949 to 1952, have thoroughly cooperated on policy, keeping political entanglements out of national finance.

The responsibility for finance and public economy falls on the shoulders of the Finance Minister, the Home Minister (an office now abolished and supplanted by that of State Minister), and the governor of the Bank of Japan. The director of the Taxation Bureau of the Ministry of Finance is directly responsible for national taxation, and the director of the Local Affairs Bureau of the Home Ministry (later, the executive director of the Local Autonomy Agency or Local Finance Commission) for local taxation. Table 14 lists those persons formerly or now in office. The month of resignation is in parentheses.

FINANCIAL AND ECONOMIC TRENDS IN RECENT YEARS

Japan was accorded the status of independence by the San Francisco Peace Treaty but her economic condition was far from stabilized. Economic stabilization was one of the most difficult problems and urgent needs that Japan had to face after the signing of the Treaty. The struggle to recover a war-shattered economy has been hard and continuous during these years. Everything considered, the economic improvement Japan has made since the Treaty is surprising, but it certainly has not been smooth sailing and very likely will not be so in the future. Efforts have been made to improve and expand production. This is necessary because of the increasing pressure of population as already explained, but it had to be done without causing the international trade balance to deteriorate.

The Korean war, which unexpectedly broke out, had a fortunate and, at the same time, an unfortunate effect on Japan's economy. It was fortunate because the influx of huge amounts of dollars into Japan, as a result of the war trade, suddenly improved the international trade balance which had been very poor up to that time. It was unfortunate because the urgent requirement of war materials boosted up general commodity prices so rapidly and so high that they were far above international price levels. When the war ended, Japan's export business suffered, and, further, the decrease in special procurement for the U. S. armed forces reduced dollar earnings and made the situation worse.

It was regrettable that, under such adverse circumstances, national finance was allowed to pursue a rather inflationary course. In order to meet various extra expenditures relating to the restoration of independence, the budget for 1952 was not the rigid "super-balanced" budget of the past. Toward the end of the year, the government found it necessary to submit a supplementary budget which included tax reductions along with disbursements of government funds, including various expenditures for consumption goods. This inflationary trend was evident also in the budget of the following year.

The 1952 budget also called for the issuance of bonds amounting to 10 billion yen to provide a fund for the newly established Industry Investment Special Account. Thus, government finance was swollen every year at every opportunity by adding new items of expenditure.

In the meantime, imports increased mainly because of a food shortage, caused by the poor crop in 1953. That year the international trade balance showed a deficit of nearly $200 million, after taking account of the invisible receipt from the special procurement, which was still as large as $800 million. The situation became alarming.

Under the circumstances, the government was forced to retrench. Money had been tightened since October, 1953, and it was promised that the budget for 1954 would be worked out within a frame of one trillion yen. The idea of reducing taxes was given up altogether and, on the whole, the government has pushed a deflationary policy. The budget for 1954 was 999.6 billion yen as compared to 1,027.3 billion yen for 1953. If we abstract a pay raise for government employees which had been in effect since January 1954, the 1954 total represents a pronounced decline in government expenditures. By these measures the government expected a decline in commodity prices of 5 to 10 percent.

After nine years in power, the Yoshida Cabinet was succeeded in December, 1954, by the Hatoyama Cabinet. Mr. H. Ichimada, who had served successfully as Governor of the Bank of Japan for nine years and as the leading figure in financial circles during those critical days, gave up the office to be succeeded by Mr. E. Araki, and he himself became the Minister of Finance. The Hatoyama Cabinet pursued the financial policy of strict economy established by its predecessor.

Fortunately, the economic condition in Japan began to improve toward the end of 1954. As a result of various anti-inflation measures, commodity prices have either remained stationary or have dropped.

The year 1955 proved to be a year of remarkable prosperity in Japan. Exports registered the second highest rate of increase in the world, yielding an overall surplus of the trade balance amounting to $500 million. An economic expansion was achieved without greatly stimulating commodity prices or credit expansion. A growth of national real income by 9% was recorded.

Prosperity was due to a global industrial boom, helped by the domestic economic improvement on account of a bumper grain crop in 1955. But real credit was due to the retrenchment policy pursued in the previous year; thereby Japan's economic condition had been so adjusted that it could take a full advantage of world industrial boom.

In December, 1956, the Hatoyama Cabinet resigned and was succeeded by the Ishibashi Cabinet. However no great change in Japan's financial policy is expected, as the new Cabinet is also one of the same conservative party—Liberal-Democrat. Mr. Araki had resigned in November, 1956, because of ill health, and was succeeded by Mr. Yamagiwa. But there should bc no marked change of policy regarding the Bank of Japan either.

One important aspect which cannot be overlooked was the progressive "normalization" of economy made during 1955. The increase in capital of various enterprises resulted in an increase of bank deposits. The prevalent and abnormal condition of overloans by the Bank of Japan to city banks was remedied to a considerable degree. In short, the stabilized economic condition which Japan has been trying to regain since the termination of war seemed to have been realized in 1955.

At the beginning of 1956, some observers were afraid that the prevailing "quantity boom" might be turned into a "price boom" and affect international trade, because the effective demand was shifting gradually from foreign sources to domestic investments. The budget for 1956 also exceeded the trillion yen mark, which had jealously been regarded as a symbol of retrenchment policy by many conservative people.

As the year went on, some people started to worry about a recessionary tendency that might develop in the near future because of overinvestment and also about a possible recession abroad. In spite of all such fears however, many people regard 1956 also as one of the most prosperous years, expecting the further growth of national income to be somewhere near 8%, although the international trade balance is going to show no surplus this year and the price level is showing a slight rise.

The world situation after the Middle East crisis seems to have once more changed the outlook of Japan's economy. Further export expansion is needed and the outlook seems bright. A word of caution, however. We must guard ourselves against an inflationary tendency. Financial as well as government circles are carefully deliberating how to handle financial problems, especially those of budget and taxation for 1957.

PART TWO

The Development of the National and Local Tax Systems

II. *The Tax Reform of 1940*

THE problem of tax reform had been a major one since 1935. It was first taken up by the Research Bureau of the Cabinet in 1935. Thereafter, during the 70th ordinary session of the Diet, convened in 1937, Dr. Baba, the Finance Minister of the Hirota Cabinet, attempted a revision of the tax system that ended in failure. The succeeding Finance Minister, Mr. Yuhki of the Hayashi Cabinet, managed to meet the urgent needs of national finance through an enactment known as the "Temporary Tax Increment Law"; this provided for a capital tax for corporations, a special tax for bonds in foreign currencies, a gasoline tax, and a securities transfer tax. At the same time, he initiated a temporary grants-in-aid fund amounting to some 100,000,000 yen, designed for the relief of local finance. Mr. Kaya, Finance Minister of the Konoe Cabinet, set up a Tax System Commission in 1937, with a view to effecting a thorough-going reform of the tax system, but his program failed to materialize, owing to the outbreak of the North China struggle, as the Sino-Japanese conflict was called in its initial stage. Mr. Kaya then proposed a North China struggle special tax, which was adopted by the 71st special session of the Diet.

As the North China struggle continued, a Special Account for Extraordinary War Expenses was created by the 72d extraordinary session of the Diet. In the 73d ordinary session in 1938, a special tax was created to replace the one of 1937. In the same session of the Diet, the extraordinary profit tax and certain other taxes were revised and the Temporary Taxation Measure Law was enacted. In a shuffle of Cabinet members, Mr. S. Ikeda succeeded Mr. Kaya as Finance Minister, but this did not lead to any further alterations in the tax system.

During the 74th ordinary session of the Diet in 1939, Mr. Ishiwata, Finance Minister of the Hiranuma Cabinet, undertook to revise the China Affair Special Tax, the Extraordinary Profit Tax, and the Temporary Taxation Measure Law. He also announced his intention to revive the Tax System Commission, which had been inactive since its inauguration in 1937. This was a prelude to a general revision of the tax system, on a national as well as a local scale.

The Tax System Commission met almost every week throughout April, May, and June, following the Diet recess in April, 1939. After August, 1939, a subcommittee made a detailed examination of a tax revision plan drawn up by the Taxation Bureau of the Ministry of Finance, and a similar proposal on the local level, drafted by the Local Affairs Bureau of the Ministry for Home Affairs. The Hiranuma Cabinet resigned in what might be regarded as a sequel to the conclusion of the Russo-German nonaggression pact. General Abe was then called upon to form a new cabinet, and Mr. Aoki was offered the portfolio of Finance. In regard to tax revision, Mr. Aoki adhered to the policy of his predecessor, Mr. Ishiwata. Following a series of some fourteen subcommittee meetings, eight plenary sessions of the Commission were called, and on October 26 a résumé of recommendations was drawn up. A tax reform plan, thus elaborated, was approved at the Cabinet meeting of December 8 and was immediately prepared for submission to the 75th session of the Diet. Upon the fall of the Abe Cabinet, Mr. Sakurauchi, Finance Minister of the incoming Yonai Cabinet introduced a reform of the tax system in the course of the 75th session of the Diet.

Various tax bills providing for fundamental reforms, national and local, were put into force from 1940 on. This far-reaching undertaking marks an important epoch in the financial history of Japan.

NATIONAL TAXATION

Extent and method of expansion. The objectives of the new reforms were 1) to secure a more equitable distribution of the burden of taxation, nationally and locally; 2) to harmonize taxation with various economic measures; 3) to establish a system that would be elastic and at the same time to ensure an increase in revenue; and 4) to simplify the tax structure as a whole. Of these goals, the third was perhaps the most important: a tax system that would be elastic and at the same time ensure an increase in revenue. Needless to say, the securing of permanent sources of revenue was of prime importance to Japan, engaged as she was in a stupendous project of long-term construction. It was not altogether impossible to increase revenues for the fiscal year 1940 by enforcing the existing tripartite enactments, consisting of the basic tax law, the Temporary Tax Increment Law, and the China Affair

Special Tax Law, but these temporary measures would be inadequate for 1941.

Therefore, any reform measures must cover expanding expenditures anticipated for the future and at the same time provide higher ordinary revenues for the current year. For these purposes, the usual suggestion would have been to create new taxes on property and business transactions or on at least one of these. The plan outlined by Dr. Baba provided for both of these. While these two taxes were not without merit, the circumstances then prevailing warranted something more useful.

Obviously, it was necessary to augment taxes if a substantial increase in revenue was to be attained, but it was a matter of careful study to determine which of the two should receive greater attention. The price policy was at the time of prime importance. It was so important, indeed, that the government, not content with fixing official prices for major commodities, had gone so far as to adopt "emergency measures for control of prices" in order to peg prices at the level of September 18, 1939.

There were exceptions to the general policy. In the case of commodities on which indirect consumption taxes were raised, a price increase was permitted. It was clear that the higher taxes would force up the prices of the commodities concerned, shifting the burden to the consumer. A big increase in excises was therefore undesirable, from the point of view of price policy. For this reason under the contemplated tax reform plan, direct taxes were to be raised to a greater extent than were indirect taxes.

The total national tax revenues for fiscal 1939, classified as direct, indirect, and other, are shown in Table 15.

Of all direct taxes the income tax was most important, accounting for 892,705,000 yen of the total, which was roughly 1,637,949,000 yen. If revenues were to be increased by placing greater weight on direct taxes, the income tax was bound to receive a lion's share of the burden.

As noted in the table, the tax revenue for 1939 was estimated at 2,940,705,000 yen, and for 1940 the estimate was expanded to 3,730,000,000 yen. Under the reform plan, the revised income tax would produce 1,500,000,000 yen, 40 percent of the total planned tax revenue. Revision of the income tax therefore constituted the nucleus of the whole plan for the new system of national taxation.

Two forms of legislation were conceivable in connection with the

TABLE 15

TOTAL DIRECT, INDIRECT, AND OTHER TAXES IN NATIONAL AND LOCAL FINANCE, 1939–1940

(In thousand yen)

Direct Taxes		*Indirect Taxes*		*Other Taxes*	
Income	892,705	Liquor	266,836	Bourse	25,234
Land	48,719	Soft drinks	8,018	Securities transfer	4,312
Business profits	126,617	Sugar excise	136,122	Tonnage dues	2,515
Capital interest	40,259	Textile excise	58,066	Stamp revenues	112,453
Corporation capital	27,807	Gasoline	10,432	Travel	11,475
Estate	61,883	Customs duties	148,796	Admission	12,307
Mining	12,783	Monopoly profits	320,219	Special admission	69
Special tax on bonds in foreign currencies	2,884	Commodity	125,879	Convertible note issue	1,154
Bourse business	2,638	Amusement, food and drinking	57,742	Building	1,127
Extraordinary profits	374,215				
Special dividends	45,658				
Special tax on public bonds and debentures	1,781				
Total	1,637,949		1,132,110		170,646
Grand total	2,940,705				

method of imposing the income tax. One was the type adopted in Germany and America: a separate levy on corporation incomes in addition to the tax imposed on individuals. The other type, in force in Britain, France, and Italy, imposed income taxes on individuals and corporations under a single tax law. Hitherto, Japanese law had provided for a mixture of both types, but the reform plan differentiated between individual and corporation income taxes. It further divided the levy on individuals into a classified and an aggregate income tax.

The classified income tax was to be imposed on incomes of all descriptions at proportionate rates, irrespective of the amount of income, while the aggregate tax was to be levied on portions of total income in excess of a stipulated amount, at progressive rates in accordance with the size of the excess. Taxing incomes of individuals on this dual basis characterizes the system of Great Britain (which has a normal or income tax and a surtax) and France (which has both the *impôts cédulaires sur les revenus* and the *impôt général sur le revenu*).

The classified income tax. The classified income tax, hitherto unknown in Japan, was to be imposed on individuals whose incomes were derived from six categories: 1) real estate; 2) dividends and interest; 3) enterprises; 4) labor services; 5) forestry operations; and 6) retirement allowances. (Corporations were also to be taxed on income from dividends and interest.)

Income from real estate was designated as accruing from land, houses, ships, and the lease of rights on real estate.

Income from dividends and interest accrued from two main categories, Class A and Class B. Class A included public bonds; corporate debentures or deposits, or profits from joint operation trusteeship received in the districts where the tax law was in operation; and dividends, profits or interest, and distribution of surplus received from corporations which had their head office or principal places of business within the enforcement area of the income tax law. Class B comprised interest on non-business loans and on public bonds, corporate debentures or deposits; profits from joint operation trusteeship; dividends, profits or interest, or allotment of surplus monies received from corporations not included in the foregoing.

Enterprises subject to income tax were divided into two groups. Group I included retail business, money-lending, commodity loan business, manufacturing, transportation, warehousing, contracting, printing, publishing, photography, hotels, restaurants, brokerage, agency, middleman enterprise, wholesale business, mining operation, alluvial mining, public bath houses, hairdressing. Group II included the professions, agriculture, stock farming and fisheries, and other enterprises not listed elsewhere.

Income from labor services included salaries, wages, annual remunerations, annuities, pensions, and other allowances of kindred nature.

Under the provisions concerning assessment, the real estate tax was to be levied on the balance after necessary expenditures were deducted from receipts. Of the sums to be distributed on liquidation of corporations, the amount exceeding the paid-up capital was to be regarded as a dividend on profits and taxed separately from other incomes. Income from enterprises constituted the balance after deducting necessary expenditure from receipts. In assessing business incomes of individuals, the extraordinary profits tax imposed on the profits for the year concerned were to be deducted. Income from labor service equaled the amount of receipts.

Stipulations concerning exemptions were these: real estate income under 250 yen would be free from taxation; a basic exemption of 500 yen would be allowed on incomes from enterprises and forestry operations; on labor service incomes there would be a basic exemption of 720 yen; and a similar exemption of 10,000 yen on incomes from retirement allowances.

Provision was made for deductions for maintenance and for life insurance premiums. For incomes from real estate, enterprises, labor services, and forestry operations, a tax amount equivalent to 8 percent of 150 yen could be deducted for each of the taxpayer's dependents, if his total income did not exceed 5,000 yen; in such cases, life insurance premiums up to 200 yen could be deducted.

The tax rate for income from real estate was set at 10 percent; for income from dividends and interest, 10 percent, except 4 percent for interest on national bonds and 9 percent for interest on local bonds. The rate for income from enterprises less than 1,000 yen was 6 percent; from commerce and industry, 8.5 percent; and from other enterprises, 7.5 percent. Income from labor service was taxed at 6 percent and from forestry at somewhat reduced rates. For retirement allowances, the rates were progressive: under 20,000 yen, 6 percent; from 20,000 yen to 100,000 yen, 12 percent; from 100,000 yen to 500,000 yen, 25 percent; over 500,000 yen, 40 percent.

The rate was 5 percent for interest on bank savings deposits, and for interest on Sangyo Kumiai (farmers' cooperative societies) when the principal exceeded 3,000 yen.

Two methods of collection were used, withholding and assessment. Income from dividends and interest derived from Class A enterprises, income from labor services and from retirement allowances, would be taxed at the source (withholding method). All other incomes would be taxed and collected, as a rule, on the basis of the actual incomes for the previous year (assessment method). A corporation drawing income from dividends or interest for which the tax had been collected at the source could deduct the amount in computing its tax.

Although the classified income tax rates were proportional, the rate for incomes from property, that is, from real estate and from dividends and interest, was fixed at 10 percent, and the rate for income from labor service at 6 percent. Intermediate rates were to be imposed on incomes from enterprises, which were regarded as accruing from property and labor services combined; that is to say, incomes from commerce and industry were to be taxed at 8.5 percent, and other incomes from enterprises at 7.5 percent. Interest on bank deposits and interest on Sangyo Kumiai savings had hitherto been exempt from taxation, but under the new system a 5 percent tax was to be imposed on them, whenever the principal involved exceeded 3,000 yen. Reduced rates of 4 percent and 9 percent, respectively, were levied on interest on national and local bonds. Just as the standard income tax rates were altered from time to time in Great Britain to meet new financial needs, so the rates of the classified income tax could be revised to meet financial exigencies. This would give elasticity to the tax system.

A basic exemption of 500 yen and 720 yen, respectively, was allowed on income from enterprises and forestry operations and from labor services, while deductions for the taxpayer's dependents and for life insurance premiums were also considered in taxing incomes from real estate, enterprises, forestry operations, and labor services. Thus, although the rates were proportional in form, they were actually more or less progressive.

Whereas, under the earlier income tax law, the withholding method of taxing at the source was applied exclusively to Class B incomes (interest on public bonds and corporate debentures, interest on bank deposits and profits from joint-operation trusteeship) and the method of lump-sum or aggregate taxation was applied to all other incomes as a general rule, under the new tax system, the withholding method was extended to practically all incomes from dividends and interest, labor services, and retirement allowances. Aggregate income taxation was confined to real estate and enterprises. As a result, the imposition of local surtaxes on the basis of the classified income tax became an impossibility. This had an important bearing on the development of a new tendency in local finance to depend on the Bunyo-Zei, Bunyo-Kin (system of grants-in-aid of taxes in the local apportionment tax system), instead of local surtaxes on the basis of national tax, as before.

The aggregate income tax. As we have seen, the classified income tax was to be imposed on incomes of all kinds at proportional rates, so as to cover the population as a whole. It did not, however, make equitable distribution of the tax burden among persons of large incomes and those of small incomes; therefore provisions were made for an aggregate income tax at progressive rates on that portion of large incomes which exceeded a specified limit. Under these provisions, incomes less that 5,000 yen were exempt from the aggregate tax. The rates for the rest were: over 5,000 yen to 8,000 yen, 10 percent; over 8,000 yen to 12,000 yen, 15 percent; over 12,000 yen to 20,000 yen, 20 percent; over 20,000 yen to 30,000 yen, 25 percent; over 30,000 yen to 50,000 yen, 30 percent; over 50,000 yen to 80,000 yen, 35 percent; over 80,000 yen to 120,000 yen, 40 percent; over 120,000 yen to 200,000 yen, 45 percent; over 200,000 yen to 300,000 yen, 50 percent; over 300,000 yen to 500,000 yen, 55 percent; over 500,000 yen to 800,000 yen, 60 percent; over 800,000 yen, 65 percent.

Incomes from interest on public bonds and corporate debentures, incomes from interest on bank deposits and from profits of joint-operation trusteeship, were to be taxed collectively, with a 40 percent deduction from receipts. For the time being, however, these incomes might be taxed at 15 percent by the withholding method on application by the taxpayer. Incomes from interest on bank savings deposits and Sangyo Kumiai savings, the principal of which exceeded 3,000 yen, would be similarly treated. In regard to dividends of profits or interest or distribution of surplus received from corporations, interest on liabilities which were necessary for acquisition of such incomes could be deducted as necessary expenditure. A 10 percent deduction could be made on incomes from labor services of persons whose total incomes were below 10,000 yen.

On all incomes, assessments were to be made, as a general rule, on the basis of actual income for the previous year.

As the aggregate income tax was at progressive rates, it was levied on the aggregate amount of the incomes accruing to individuals from various sources. The method of imposition was, on the whole, the same as that applied to the earlier Class III income tax, except in the following three respects. First, whereas a 20 percent deduction had hitherto been allowed for dividends on shares, regardless of any indebtedness of the taxpayer, this deduction was abolished with a proviso that where the taxpayers contracted a debt in acquiring the shares, interest on the debt could be deducted as necessary expenditure from incomes. Secondly, in the case of interest on public bonds and corporate debentures, or interest on bank deposits and on profits of joint-operation trusteeships, or incomes falling under the category of Class II incomes under the earlier tax law, a 40 percent deduction was allowed. Thirdly, since incomes of this kind had hitherto been taxed at the source by the withholding method, some apprehension was felt that a sudden change-over to collective taxation might cause much inconvenience; consequently, as a transitional arrangement, the way was kept open so that, if the taxpayer chose, these incomes would be taxed by the withholding method at the proportional rate of 15 percent.

Since the progressive rates applied only to the excess amount of income, they were graded moderately, up to the maximum of 65 percent. In an extreme case, an income might be taxable at 75 percent, that is, 10 percent under the classified tax plus 65 percent under the aggregate tax. When this fact was taken into consideration, it would readily be seen that a local surtax could not be imposed.

The corporation tax and the special corporation tax. A separate corporation tax was created, chiefly along the lines of the income tax and partly along the lines of the capital tax.

When the corporation tax was imposed, the Class I income tax, the corporation business profits tax, and the former corporation capital tax were abolished (the excess income tax was incorporated in the extraordinary profit tax).

The corporation tax was imposed on income accrued during every accounting period, on liquidation income, and on the capital of corporations. In assessing corporation income, the corporation tax could not be counted as loss, but the amount of loss incurred in the previous three business years could. The assessed income constituted the balance after deduction from total income of the extraordinary profit tax imposed on profits for the business year. The rates were 18 percent of the amount of income and 1.5 per mille of the capital.

In the case of a corporation lacking either a head office or principal places of business within the enforcement area of the corporation tax law, the rate was 28 percent of the amount of income. The tax could not be levied on that portion of liquidation income which consisted of reserve funds and untaxable income. The classified income tax on dividends and interest accruing to corporations could be deducted from the corporation tax.

What is particularly noteworthy about the corporation tax is the revision that was made in the method of calculation. According to the revised method (as said before) the corporation tax was not to be counted as loss in assessing incomes of corporations, while the amount of loss incurred in the previous three business years could be included in losses when assessing the income for the current business year. Whereas the latter revision operated to lighten the burden of corporations, the former was bound to add to it. Theoretically speaking, it is correct to exclude the income tax in the calculation of loss, as corporation income is regarded as gross profit minus gross loss, and the corporation tax is supposed to be imposed on the remainder. But since the corporation tax had hitherto been included in the loss, the new method of calculation would inevitably lead to considerable increase in the tax burden of corporations during the period of transition. The rates were calculated on a two-fold basis: 18 percent of income and 1.5 per mille of capital.

The second objective of the new tax reform plan was "to harmonize taxation with the various economic measures," among which an expansion of productive power was regarded as of particular importance. Inasmuch as corporations have a very important part to play in this respect, the Ministry of Finance requested the five points be incorporated in the tax system, to facilitate expansion: 1) a reduction in taxes on income reserved for acquiring new equipment or for purchase of national bonds; 2) a reduction of rates on the incomes from enterprises abroad; 3) the exemption of important minerals from the income tax, the corporation tax, and the business tax, in the initial year of mining operation and also for the next three years, similar to the exemptions granted to industries manufacturing certain essential articles; 4) a curtailing of the period of depreciation allowed for fixed assets devoted to wartime industries where old plants were involved; 5) a differentiation of industrial companies run by family groups and some reduction of the rates of taxes.

The special corporation tax was imposed on special corporations such as Sangyo Kumiai, commercial associations, the federation of commercial associations, industrial associations, the federation of industrial associations, the central bank of Sangyo Kumiai, and the central bank of commercial and industrial associations. It was also imposed on the surplus funds of special corporations (the surplus fund reserved for payment as dividends being excepted). Sangyo Kumiai, commercial associations, and industrial associations whose surplus funds fell short of a certain fixed percentage of paid-up contributions were exempt. The rate of the tax was 6 percent of surplus funds.

The extraordinary profit tax and the estate tax. Of the revisions of national taxes other than the income tax, the revision of the extraordinary profit tax deserves special attention. This tax developed out of the Class A excess profit tax (an impost on a portion exceeding the average profit for the three years 1929, 1930, and 1931), which was created at the time of the Manchurian struggle, and the Class B excess profit tax (an impost on a portion exceeding the average profits for the three years 1934, 1935, and 1936), which came into being as a sequel to the China struggle; they were later incorporated in one. Under the new tax reform plan, the Class A tax was abolished and the Class B retained.

The new extraordinary profit tax applied to individuals as well as to corporations. In regard to corporations, the extraordinary profit tax and the excess income tax were to be concurrently imposed on corporations. For the amount of profit exceeding the standard rate of profit or the amount exceeding 10 percent per annum of the capital (inclusive of reserve funds), the rate was 25 percent on the portion exceeding 10 percent per annum of the capital but falling short of the standard rate of profit. It was 45 percent on the portion exceeding the standard rate of profit but falling short of 30 percent per annum of the capital, and 65 percent on the portion exceeding 30 percent per annum of the capital. For corporations with capital of less than 100,000 yen, these rates were reduced by 10 percent. The standard rate of profit for corporations was set at the average for the three years 1934, 1935, and 1936. Where the average was unavailable, or when it was below 10 percent, the standard rate of profit was fixed at 10 percent per annum. If the average rate of profit exceeded 20 percent per annum, the standard rate of profit was fixed at 20 percent per annum. In assessing profits, the corporation tax and the extraordinary profit tax could not be calculated as loss.

As applied to individuals, the Class A excess profit tax was abolished and a portion of profit in excess of the average profit for the three years

1934, 1935, and 1936 became the taxable profit, and the extraordinary profit tax was imposed on this portion at the rate of 30 percent.

For persons who either had no average profit to go by or whose average profit was less than one-third of the profit for the current fiscal year, the arbitrary figure of 7,000 yen (even if the actual amount was less than that) was set as the average profit.

The extraordinary profit tax was not imposed if profits of individuals for the current fiscal year were less than 10,000 yen. In assessing profits of individuals, the income tax and the extraordinary profit tax were not to be calculated as necessary expenditures.

The extraordinary profit tax for corporations was a combination of corporation excess income tax and the Class B excess profit tax. The maximum progressive rate of 65 percent might be considered a heavy burden on the financial world. But this burden might be somewhat alleviated by the regulation, according to which the extraordinary profit tax, levied on the profit for the year concerned, was to be deducted in assessing business profits of individuals, and the regulation by which the extraordinary profit tax, levied on the profit of the corporation for the year concerned, was to be deducted in assessing the corporation tax, so that the aggregate income tax or corporation tax would be imposed on the balance.

The chief features of the estate tax were: 1) an increase of some 30 percent in the total revenue from the tax; and 2) under Class A succession to the headship of the house in which the value of property to be inherited was less than 50,000 yen, a deduction of 1,000 yen for each member of the family depending upon the heritor for support.

The liquor tax, the sugar excise, the commodity tax, and the amusement, eating and drinking tax. Along with the revisions of the direct national taxes on incomes, on extraordinary profits, and on estates, revisions were made affecting a group of indirect consumption taxes.

All tax laws regarding liquors (the sake-manufacturing tax law, the alcoholic and spiritous beverages tax law, the beer tax law, and the provisions for the China struggle special tax law in reference to liquors) were unified into a single tax law. The amount of brewage or the amount carried out of breweries was taxed, according to different qualities of liquors. An equitable incidence of tax burden was insured for liquors of different qualities. In general, the multifarious imposts to which liquors had hitherto been subjected were coordinated, and the revenue from this source was increased by 30 percent.

Under the soft drinks tax, the total revenue from the tax on all soft drinks except Tama-Ramune (bottled lemonade) was increased by some 30 percent.

The sugar excise provided a change in the standard for fixing tax rates from shades of color to the methods of manufacture and increased the total tax revenue by some 20 percent.

The textile excise law increased the tax rate from 9 percent to 10 percent and adjusted the scope of exemption.

The gasoline tax rate was raised by 8 sen per gallon.

The travel tax was extended to third-class passenger fares for journeys by rail or by ship covering a distance of less than 50 kilometers but more than 40 kilometers. The rate was raised from three to ten sen for third-class passengers, and the express train charge was taxed at 10 percent.

The admissions tax and the special admissions tax stipulated that the exemption to limit for admission fees for theaters, cinema halls, etc., should be lowered from 23 sen to 19 sen, while the rate for admission fees over one yen was increased to some extent. The rate for admission fees for dance halls and golf links was also somewhat higher. The exemption limit in the special admission tax was lowered from 23 sen to 19 sen.

The commodity tax was newly imposed on ivory wares, cloisonné wares, amber articles, fine confections, pets, and potted plants. The rate for commodities falling under the categories of Class A and Class B, Section 1, was raised from 15 percent to 20 percent, and the rate for wheat-gluten was raised by 50 sen per 100 kin. The scope of the tax was extended, though not to such an extent as to render it virtually a tax on proceeds of sales. The revision was confined to the increase of rates for commodities of pronouncedly luxury items.

Under the amusement, eating and drinking tax, the tax rate for tips for geisha was raised from 20 percent to 30 percent and the rate for tips to other employees and on other charges was raised from 10 percent to 15 percent. At the same time the exemption point was lowered from 5 yen to 3 yen. No exemption was provided for charges accompanied by tips for geisha and for charges at cafes.

The land tax, the house tax, and the business tax. The land tax was left intact, the business profit tax was renamed the business tax, and the house tax, which had hitherto been a prefectural tax, was made a national tax. All three were transformed into national taxes.

The standards of assessment were: for the land tax, on the basis of the rental value of land under the current Land Tax Law; for the house tax, on the basis of the rental value of houses as set by a recent official inquiry; for the business tax, in the case of individuals, on the basis of incomes assessed for the purpose of imposing the classified income tax and in the case of corporations on the basis of incomes assessed in connection with the imposition of the corporation tax.

The land tax rate was fixed at 2 percent, the house tax at 1.75 percent, the business tax at 1.50 percent. The revenues from these taxes were granted to the prefecture in which they were collected.

Opinion had long been divided as to whether the land and the business taxes should be transferred to local treasuries with a view toward making all three profit taxes local taxes, or whether, on the other hand, the house tax should be transferred to the national treasury, so as to make them all national taxes. The latter course was now decided upon. Simultaneously, it was decided to return these revenues to the prefectures where they were collected, instead of using them for purposes of national finance, and the controversy which had been carried on for some years was amicably settled.

LOCAL TAXATION

Generally speaking, there had been no interflow between national and local finance, with the exception of subsidies granted for specific purposes. National taxes were designed to provide funds to administer national finance, while local taxes were expected to provide for local needs. It was not until a state subsidy for compulsory education (a quasi-grant-in-aid for local finance) was granted that any ties were forged between national and local finance. These ties became closer when temporary grants-in-aid were created to relieve local finance. Thereupon the question of promoting harmony between national and local taxes began to attract a great deal of attention. The abolition, under the new tax reform plan, of the local surtax hitherto levied on the income tax (the most important direct national tax) made reform of the local tax system imperative.

Special attention was directed to the creation of a new system for the distribution of tax revenues. Other noteworthy measures were the surtaxes on land, house, and business taxes; the independent prefectural taxes; the municipal, town, and village surtaxes imposed upon the taxes; and also the independent municipal, town, or village taxes. The municipal, town, and village taxes were created with a view to fostering among their inhabitants an attitude of cooperation in sharing the burden of taxation. In extending the scope of the special purpose tax and the system of beneficiaries' shares in the cost of undertakings, it might also be noted that the intention was to stimulate local enterprise. Lastly, it was planned to redistribute the burden of taxation between national and local finance through adjustments of subsidies. The detailed explanations are given below.

Grants-in-aid (system of local apportionment tax). The system of grants-in-aid for distribution of tax revenues not only served to put local finance on a secure basis, but tended to eliminate financial inequalities among local governments. The underlying idea had already been demonstrated in the state subsidy for compulsory education, and it was further strongly expressed in temporary grants-in-aid for relief of local finance. However, the temporary nature of these grants emphasized the need for more permanent sources of revenue at the local level. The new grants-in-aid system was constituted to meet this need.

Taxes for distribution as sources of grants-in-aid (chiho bunyo zei; local apportionment tax) were of two kinds, refund taxes and distributive taxes.

Refund taxes (kanpu-zei) comprised land, house, and business taxes. All prefectures benefited through the return of the taxes to the prefectures where they were collected.

Distributive taxes (haifu-zei) comprised a portion of the income, corporation, amusement, and admission taxes, to the benefit of prefectures, cities, towns, and villages. The object of apportionment of these taxes was to enable local public bodies to meet their respective financial needs through aid from the central government, when local sources of revenue were inadequate. Consequently, the standard of apportionment was decided according to financial capacity and needs.

The tax-bearing capacity in terms of the land tax, the house tax, and the business tax was considered a criterion of financial capacity, and apportionments were to be made in inverse proportion to it. The size of population was a criterion of the extent of financial needs, and apportionments were to be made in direct proportion to population.

In the transitional period, to preclude violent changes which might arise in the finances of public bodies if there was a decline in the amount of revenues, caused by the tax reform itself, apportionments were to be made in direct proportion to possible decline.

It was recognized that the basic rules for apportionment should be laid down by law, and that a committee consisting mostly of members of both Houses of the Diet should be set up to ensure the equitable distribution of revenues. Appropriate methods had to be devised to ensure apportionments of taxes in the manner best calculated to meet the local financial needs at suitable periods in the fiscal year. As has been noted, the refund taxes (kanpu-zei) were to be turned over to the prefectures where they had been collected by the government as national taxes.

The distributive tax (haifu-zei) comprised 16.55 percent of the classified income tax, the aggregate income tax, and the corporation tax; and 50 percent of the amusement tax and the admission tax, amounting in all to some 350,000,000 yen. In apportioning the taxes, financial capacity of the local government was to be calculated on the basis of the average amount per item of the objects of taxation for the three profit taxes.

The methods of distribution were practically the same as those adopted in distributing the temporary grants-in-aid for the relief of local finance, the amount was some 148,000,000 yen. An important consideration was the adjustment of the portion allotted to local public bodies and that assigned to special local objectives.

Surtaxes on national taxes. Prefectures, cities, towns, and villages were permitted to impose surtaxes on taxes nationally assessed on land, houses, businesses, and mine lots. A certain degree of leeway was allowed in the surtax rates on all of these but mine lots, so as to ensure elasticity in the financing of local bodies. These rates were to be uniform within the local civic unit.

The rate of the prefectural land surtax was set at 100 percent and that of the city, town, or village land surtax at 200 percent of the land tax. The land surtax was to be imposed even on small lots of farm land, except those of an assessed rental value of less than 200 yen. The rate of the prefectural house surtax was to be 100 percent and that of the city, town, or village house surtax 200 percent of the house tax. The rate of the prefectural business surtax was 100 percent and that of the city, town or village business surtax 200 percent of the business tax.

The restrictive limit of the prefectural, city, town, or village mine lot surtax was 10 percent of the mine lot tax.

Among the surtaxes on national taxes, those imposed on land, house, and business taxes deserve special attention. Since the prefectures could impose surtaxes equivalent to the principal national taxes and also receive these taxes in the form of the refund tax, they actually would receive double the amount of the national taxes. The smaller civic units would also realize double the amount of these three national taxes in the form of surtaxes. Thus, the revenues of all the local units would be equitable.

Two points should be mentioned. In the first place, the surtax rates were not necessarily a maximum, for a way was left open to increase them beyond this limit. It was, indeed, just possible that the rates might prove to be a minimum—an advantage from the point of view of elasticity.

In the second place, we must consider whether it was right to divide the revenues from these three national taxes in equal proportions among the prefectures, cities, towns, and villages, and particularly whether the same method of distribution should be applied to the six great cities and their prefectures and to all other cities, towns, and villages, and their respective prefectures.

Independent prefectural taxes and surtaxes imposed upon them by cities, towns, and villages. In addition to the surtaxes on national taxes, prefectures were permitted to impose independent taxes, and a portion of the current miscellaneous taxes were to be transferred to city, town, and village treasuries (the designation "miscellaneous tax" was abolished). The independent taxes were limited to acreage, vessels, automobiles, electric poles, real property acquisition, fishing rights, hunters, and geisha.

The acreage tax was to be imposed on land otherwise exempt from taxation, on the basis of the assessed rental value and in the same way as the land surtax was levied. The vessel tax was to be imposed exclusively on vessels of over 20 gross tons. Some reductions were considered in respect to the automobile tax. The fishing rights tax was to be imposed either directly on fishing rights or on the acquisition of those rights. The special land tax was to be abolished.

Cities, towns, and villages could impose surtaxes not only on national taxes but on the independent prefectural taxes listed above. The rate of these surtaxes was 100 percent of the principal taxes, with some margin of elasticity, and were to be uniform within the same city, town, and village.

Independent city, town, and village taxes. In addition to the surtaxes which they were entitled to impose on national and prefectural taxes, cities, towns, and villages were permitted independent taxes as follows: inhabitant's tax, boat tax, bicycle tax, cart tax, safe tax, electric fan tax, butchery tax, dog tax, other miscellaneous taxes.

They were allowed to impose any taxes given in the list of independent prefectural taxes that were not already imposed by the prefectures. They could also levy taxes of their own devising, subject to the approval of the national government officials.

The specified taxes could be imposed in the same way that miscellaneous taxes had been imposed, with certain exceptions. Persons on public or private relief were exempt from the inhabitant's tax. It was levied on households, and on residing individuals, not in households, who were self-supporting; on persons with a business office in the local district; and on corporations with a business office in the district. The date of collection was to be uniform throughout the country, and the methods of collection were to be as simple as possible, with regard to local conditions.

The average maximum amount per head was fixed at 8 yen in cities with a population of over 700,000, at 6 yen in other cities, and at 4 yen in towns and villages. The highest amount which could be imposed was fixed at 2,000 yen in cities with a population of over 700,000 and at 1,000 yen in all other localities.

The boat tax was imposed on ships of less than 20 tons gross. The bicycle tax could be reduced to some extent.

One noteworthy fact in regard to the independent city, town, and village taxes was that the much-criticized kosuwari (household rate) was abolished in favor of the inhabitant's tax. This was wider in scope than the kosuwari, for it applied equally to absentee landowners and corporations. On the other hand, it was restrictive in that the average amount per head was fixed at 8 yen in the six great cities, 6 yen in all other cities and 4 yen in towns and villages, and that the maximum amount of impost was fixed at 2,000 yen in the six great cities and at 1,000 yen in all other localities. Special care had to be taken in enforcing the tax in the six great cities, for the kosuwari had not been imposed in them because of the constant shifting about of city people; the income surtax and the excess rates of the house tax were imposed instead.

The special purpose tax and beneficiaries' contributions to the cost of undertakings. The fixed rates of the taxes described above seriously inconvenienced local public bodies in launching new undertakings, even at the cost of higher taxation. It was therefore decided to inaugurate the special purpose tax and consonantly a system by which beneficiaries of projects would share in the costs.

The special purpose tax was adjusted and extended to augment the city planning special tax levied chiefly for the benefit of urban districts, and to assist cooperative undertakings, chiefly for the benefit of agricultural communities. In regard to the city planning special tax, a part of the prefectural taxes was to be transferred to cities, towns, and villages, with careful equalization of the rates.

The imposition of the chiso-wari (allotment on land tax) and the tanbetsu-wari (allotment on acreage tax) was permitted in order to provide funds for the promotion of irrigation and other projects to increase productivity of land. Opportunity was given for cities, towns, and villages to create new taxes to finance cooperative workshops and storehouses and other types of cooperative enterprise.

Regarding the system by which beneficiaries would share in the cost of undertakings, the principle was laid down that all beneficiaries should contribute their share not only to building costs but to maintenance costs as well. If the special purpose tax and the system relating to beneficiaries were conceived rationally and operated successfully, sufficient margin would be afforded for the development of municipal finance.

A summary of the various prefectural and city, town, and village taxes is presented at the end of this chapter.

State subsidies for compulsory education and police expenditures borne jointly by national and local treasuries. State subsidies form a link between national and local finance, but they had never been systemized in Japan, because they had been brought into being as expedients to meet special needs as these arose. In this general reform of the tax system, the state subsidy for compulsory education, which was typical of all subsidies, and the system for the joint disbursement of police expenditures by national and local treasuries were to be revised as follows.

Salaries for primary school teachers would be paid out of prefectural treasuries and the state subsidy for compulsory education would be distributed uniformly. The proportions of police expenditures disbursed jointly would be harmonized.

The state subsidy for compulsory education had been distributed more liberally to towns and villages than to cities and to poorer localities than to those better off. It thus happened that for certain cities enjoying ordinary prosperity the subsidy might represent approximately 20 percent of the payroll for primary school teachers, whereas for some of the poorer towns and villages it might be 100 percent of these payrolls. Under the new plan, prefectures would be granted a uniform rate of approximately 50 percent of the payroll, thereby divesting the state subsidy of the nature of a grant-in-aid. It appeared, however, that the six great cities were opposed, from an educational point of view, to the plan which provided payment of primary school teachers' salaries out of the prefectural treasuries.

The burden of police expenditures fell with exceptional weight on the Tokyo and Osaka urban prefectures, and it was now proposed to coordinate these disbursements on a uniform basis.

SUMMARY OF PREFECTURAL AND CITY, TOWN, AND VILLAGE TAXES, 1940

Kind of Tax	*Prefectural*	*City, Town, and Village*
Local Tax Revenues		
Ordinary		
Surtax on national tax	land, house, business, mine lot	land, house, business, mine lot
Surtax on prefectural		acreage, vessel, automobile, electric pole, real property, fishing, hunting, geisha
Independent	acreage, vessel, automobile, electric pole, real property, fishing, hunting, geisha	inhabitants, boat, bicycle, cart, safe, electric fan, butchery, dog, misc.
Special purpose		
City planning	allotment on land, house, business, and prefectural independent taxes	allotment on land, house, business, prefectural independent, municipal independent, and misc. taxes
Water utility and land profit	allotment on land and acreage taxes	allotment on land and acreage taxes
Common facilities		at city, town, or village level only
Local Apportionment Revenues		
Distributive	portion of income, corporation, amusement, and admissions taxes	portion of income, corporation, amusement, and admissions taxes
Refund	total land, house, and business taxes	

III. *Tax Reforms during World War II*

THE tax reform of 1940 was undertaken to reorganize a patchwork of laws, promulgated one after the other with little coordination, and to establish a workable wartime tax structure. The revision of 1941, therefore, needed no more than slight structural changes, after World War II was declared in December, 1941, and the rapid expansion of the war theater demanded ever-increasing expenditures. Instead, only technical procedures such as widening the assessment basis and raising the tax rates were necessary. It must be pointed out that, although the revision of 1940 was designed for wartime, the continuous vast outlay for war expenditures was completely unforeseen, as only a short war was anticipated. At first the government believed that the bulk of the war funds could be raised through bonds or borrowings.

What characterized public finance, then, was a sharp expansion of war expenditures. The details of the Special Account for Extraordinary

TABLE 16

WAR EXPENSES AND THEIR SOURCES
(SPECIAL ACCOUNT FOR EXTRAORDINARY WAR EXPENSES)

(In million yen)

		Receipts			
Year	*Disbursements*	*Transfers from General Account*	*Bonds*	*Borrowings*	*Total (Including Others)*
1937	2,034		1,440		1,481
1938	4,795	1	3,672		3,811
1939	4,844	317	3,898		4,309
1940	5,722	1,135	5,046		6,334
1941	9,487	1,078	6,876		8,150
1942	18,753	2,623	12,564		15,888
1943	29,818	4,369	17,538	5,297	28,697
1944	73,493		23,809	34,218	59,687
1945	16,464	7,205	32,260	3,166	44,945
Total	165,410	16,728	107,103	42,681	173,302

War Expenses given in Table 16 show how these were met. Transfers from the General Account, composed chiefly of tax receipts, were very small, whereas receipts from bond issues were large. Attention is called particularly to the fact that borrowings were added to the sources of treasury funds in 1943.

To curb the inflationary tendency which emerged as a result of increasing government bonds and borrowings, the controls over commodity prices and distribution were strengthened, and an attempt was made to absorb surplus purchasing power by inducing people to buy government bonds and by encouraging them to save. The fact that these measures were successful, at least on the surface, in checking inflation, illustrates not only the ability of the Japanese people to endure hardship but also the power of the central government.

Military affairs were accorded strict priority and the national policy of unification reduced local governments to mere agencies of the state. It was unnecessary to make any adjustment in local revenues because all local public undertakings had to be deferred. Only a minimum adjustment of grants by the central government to local bodies was included in the reform.

REVISION OF DECEMBER, 1941

As stated above, the overall reform of 1940 was aimed at the reorganization of the tax system into a wartime structure to secure a greater flexibility of revenue sources for the purpose of meeting the treasury's mounting war requirements. However, the war, ignited by the German invasion of Poland in September, 1939, developed into a series of crises: the American and British participation; the surrender of France, and the conclusion of the Tripartite Alliance among Japan, Germany, and Italy in 1940, followed by the British and American freezing of Japanese assets in 1941. As the clouds of war drew nearer, Japan was compelled to speed up her armament program, and the treasury requirements increased by leaps and bounds.

The plan to increase tax rates, under consideration since the beginning of 1941, was now partially put in force chiefly in the field of indirect taxes, with the double objective of increasing revenues and curbing the purchasing power of the public. The revision called for an increase of the tax rates on liquor (chiefly delivery), soft drinks, sugar, commodities (broadened in scope), amusement, eating and drinking, admissions, travel, building, playing sets (meaning playing cards—ordinary cards or original Japanese playing cards—and mah-jong sets; the word in Japanese is *koppai-zei*), and stamps. The prices of monopoly tobacco and alcohol were also raised. Additional revenue was estimated at 214 million yen for fiscal 1941 and at 792 million yen for a full normal year. The increase in the rates of the amusement, eating and drinking tax was as high as 250 percent. The rate of the distributive tax (one of the classifications of the apportionment taxes to be granted to the local governments), of the amusement, eating and drinking tax, and the admissions tax was actually lowered, on the ground that local finance should not receive benefits from the broadly increased receipts from these taxes.

REVISION OF APRIL, 1942

As a modern war on a vast scale, World War II required unprecedented expenditures. Government spending increased at a rapid pace, the government was hurriedly compelled to enforce tax increase measures in full scale that had been under deliberation since the preceding year, implementing the classified income taxes as its nucleus.

In contrast to the revision of 1941 which dealt with indirect taxes, the revision of 1942 principally sought an increase in direct taxes, with the exception of certain indirect taxes not included in the revision of 1941. The creation of taxes on electricity and gas, horse-racing, and advertisements was new.

From the outset of the war, government funds began to flood the market, and many monetary difficulties were anticipated. To insure smooth operation of the war economy, the government promulgated a Wartime Emergency Monetary Measure immediately after the declaration of war, in order to absorb floating purchasing power and also to restrain nonessential consumption; at the same time several exceptional arrangements were provided for in the tax system for the same purpose.

Of the three newly created taxes, that on electricity and gas was imposed at the rate of 10 percent of service charge over 3 yen per month for electricity or gas used at residences, shops, hotels, and theaters. The electric power and gas suppliers added the tax to the monthly regular bills and paid the amount to the government the following month.

For the sake of easy collection and classification, the sources for the advertisement tax were divided into two groups, the first including publications in newspapers, magazines, books, and transportation facilities, and the second covering posters, signboards, hand-bills, and the like.

The first group was subject to an ad valorem imposition at the rate of 10 percent; the tax on the second group was imposed on a specific basis, depending on the kind of advertisement. In the case of the first group, the advertisers themselves were required to pay the tax whereas for advertisements in the second group, stamps were usually affixed in lieu of tax payment, with the exception of hand-bills and the like, for which payment was to be made by the producers.

The standard of assessment of the horse-racing tax was either the proceeds of sales of race tickets or the amount of rebates paid on the tickets, the rate of the tax ranging from 4 percent to 20 percent. The sponsors of races were responsible for payment of the tax.

Total revenues from the electricity and gas, advertisements, and horse-racing taxes were estimated at 63 million yen for fiscal 1942 and at 69 million yen for a subsequent normal fiscal year.

Of the existing taxes, those which were revised included direct taxes (income tax, corporation tax, extraordinary profit tax, special corporation tax, and estate tax) and indirect taxes (the textile excise, commodity tax, and stamp tax). The principal changes in the income tax were 1) in the classified tax, lowering the exemption limit and raising the allowable dependency credit and life insurance premium deductions and raising rates all around; 2) in the aggregate tax, revising income brackets and raising the progressive rates. In regard to the corporation tax, a rise in the general rates and an additional tax for family corporations were stipulated. Revenue from the extraordinary profit tax was also raised by changing brackets and rates. Other outstanding changes were the higher rates for the estate tax and textile excise, and the increase in allowable dependency credit. The total revenues from all these changes, including those from the three new taxes, were estimated at as much as 973 million yen for fiscal 1942 and 1,155 million yen for a full normal year. In enforcing the tax increases, in coordination with the various wartime economic policies, special consideration was given to the matter of exceptional tax reduction or exemption by revising the Emergency Taxation Measures Law, and also by special legislation for war disaster.

Reduction or exemption under the Emergency Taxation Measures Law was applied to: persons whose businesses were suspended because of dissolution or merger compelled by industrial mobilization; employment of undivided profits for an expansion of productive equipment; dividends on newly subscribed stocks of war enterprises; interest on bank deposits, government bonds, and corporate debentures.

The reduction of tax rates for interest on deposits, bonds and debentures was designed to foster the issuing of bonds that characterized Japan's war finance and to keep a check on inflation. In other words, preferential treatment was given to deposits to encourage financial institutions to buy government bonds, which were at first purchased wholly by the Bank of Japan. While this arrangement was in no way original with the 1942 revision, it was nevertheless regarded as one of its outstanding features. Besides the foregoing, it cannot be overlooked that the law preventing overlapping taxation in Japan and Manchuria introduced into the tax system of Japan, for the first time, the principle of reciprocal international taxation, although a similar principle had been practiced for vessels for some time in the past. Along with the revision of the income tax and the corporation tax, the rate of distributive tax to local governments (based on the income tax and corporate tax) was reduced, whereas the rate based on the admission tax and the amusement, eating, and drinking tax was raised somewhat.

REVISION OF APRIL, 1943

In 1942 Japanese forces advanced to the Aleutians, the Philippines, Malay, the East Indies and New Guinea, and occupied these areas for the time. As the war gradually assumed the aspect of a prolonged affair, Japan's war expenses mounted in geometric progression. Again the government was forced to revise taxes upward, and again indirect taxes were chiefly affected. Particularly high rates were imposed on luxury items, a step appropriate to the stabilizing of wartime living, and to the tax-bearing capacity of the people. Moreover, a wise policy was followed in granting a special, though limited, ration of sake (rice wine) and tobacco at low cost to workers in key industries, and, at the same time, strengthening the controls over production and distribution of these commodities. Prices of goods subjected to the increased indirect taxes were permitted to rise in proportion to the tax increase, despite the extension of price controls over a wide range of items.

The rates affected by the upward revision were the liquor tax, soft drink tax, transaction tax, sugar excise, commodity tax, amusement, eating and drinking tax, admissions tax, extraordinary profit tax and a newly created special act tax. Additional revenues from these sources, together with the monopoly profit from the higher tobacco prices, were estimated at 1,454 million yen for fiscal 1943 and 1,592 million yen for a normal year.

The special act tax was levied on such businesses as printing, bookbinding, dyeing and processing of textiles and garments, hair-cutting, hair-dressing, and photography, the rates ranging from 20 percent to 30 percent of the charges. Receipts from this tax were estimated at 65 million yen for fiscal 1943 and 71 million yen for a normal year. The liquor tax was again raised on the basis of delivery, but in consideration of tax-bearing capacity, sake was classified into four grades, with a different increase in rate for each. The increase of other tax rates was fairly pronounced. The domestic tax exemption system and the grant system, favoring exports to foreign countries or Korea, were abolished, partly because they were no longer warranted and partly to simplify the tax administration. The apportionment rate of the local grant was again reduced for the same reason as before.

In parallel with the upward revisions of the tax rates, the scope of the Temporary Taxation Measures Law was expanded in relation to industrial reorganizations. Since the repeated tax increases had become a considerable burden on the people, the Tax Payment Facilities Law was enacted to make payments easier. The law, providing summary procedures for tax-paying organizations, corporation reserves for taxes, and deposits for tax payments, was concurrently designed to stimulate savings.

REVISION OF APRIL, 1944

In 1943, the counteroffensives of the Allied forces were turned loose on a full scale, and being completely defeated in the southeastern Pacific, the Aleutian, and the Marshall Islands, the Japanese forces suffered a steady setback on all fronts. In the European theater, the German armies failed in their operations in Russia, and Italy finally surrendered. Notwithstanding these adverse developments, Japan still occupied a major portion of southeastern Asia and still believed that she held an advantageous position; it was decided to push the wartime financial structure further in the hope of eventual victory through total mobilization of economic strength. The government then effected the most radical increase ever attempted, in the rates of both direct and indirect taxes. Not only were the rates revised upward, but the scope of assessment was extended and, at the same time, an attempt was made to simplify the system as far as possible. For example, forestry income was moved from the aggregate income category to the classified income group; small taxpayers were permitted to pay in two instalments; the liquor tax was made collectible singly on the basis of deliveries, and the tax on brewing was abolished. To relieve deteriorating local finance caused by increased expenses for air defense and military relief, the rates were increased on land, house, and business taxes, for which local governments were entitled to full refund from the central government; on the other hand, the rate of the distributive tax to the local governments was reduced, on the basis of the greatly increased revenue from the income tax and others.

The taxes affected by the 1944 revision were the income tax, the corporation tax, the special corporation tax, the business tax, the extraordinary profit tax, the special tax on dividends and interest, the land and house tax, the estate tax, the traveling tax, the registration tax, the liquor tax, the soft drinks tax, the sugar excise, the textile excise, the commodity tax, the amusement, eating and drinking tax, the admissions tax, the special act tax, the advertisement tax, the playing-sets tax, and the stamp tax. Additional receipts from these were estimated at 2,800 million yen for fiscal 1944 and 3,100 million yen for a normal year, including the additional monopoly profit resulting from the advanced tobacco prices enforced simultaneously.

REVISION OF APRIL, 1945

Adverse developments in 1944 made Japan's defeat convincingly apparent. By a series of offensives from the occupation of Saipan Island to the landing in the Philippines, United States forces penetrated the Pacific from east to west, and in the same year initiated attacks on the Japanese homeland with long-range bombers. It became an open secret that there was a glaring shortage of materials and everything else in the country. After 1944 when the production peak was recorded, the pace slacked off, although the total economic strength continued to be poured into war production. In the financial phase, another attempt was made to increase taxes to augment treasury revenues and absorb the purchasing power of the people. The government was forced to realize that taxable sources had already reached bottom. What could be done was to try to increase taxes in a simplified and selective manner under the existing tax system, always taking into consideration the tax-bearing limit and always seeking to avoid confusion in the tax administration. With this in mind, the revision was limited to the classified income tax only, in the field of income tax, together with the corporation tax, the special corporation tax, the travel tax, the liquor tax, the amusement, eating and drinking tax, the admissions tax, and the playing-sets tax. Locally, the inhabitant tax was raised and the rate of the distributive tax to the local bodies was revised accordingly.

Among the changes, the most outstanding was a partial adoption of the self-assessment system in regard to the corporation tax and other taxes which had formerly been assessed by tax offices. To avoid delay in treasury receipts because of the slow assessment of corporation taxes, and to reduce the inconvenience to corporations caused by the delay, corporations with a capital of 5 million yen or more (and some other specific corporations) were required to submit their declarations and to pay their taxes within two months following the regular closing of their accounts (on which the taxes were calculated), subject to later adjustment by the tax office. Payment was simplified for certain items; the income tax became payable twice a year, the land tax once a year, and the individual extraordinary profit tax twice a year. The simplification of the tax-levying method also included a reduction in the number of classifications in the liquor tax, abolition of the special sake ration, imposition at a single straight rate on lodging charges and meal charges at amusement, eating and drinking places, and omission of stamps used for payment of the playing-sets tax.

Increased receipts from these taxes were estimated at 1,923 million yen for fiscal 1945 and at 1,805 million yen for a normal year. In addition, estimated increase of the monopoly profit due to the raised tobacco prices reached 690 million yen. Besides these changes, the State Tax Reduction and Exemption Law for War-afflicted Persons was revised to allow some leeway in the investigation and determination of assessment standard for war-afflicted persons who deserved urgent and special treatment.

REVISION OF AUGUST, 1945

As the disaster of war spread over the mainland, Japan's economy was thrown into utter confusion, and emergency financial expedients were adopted in the form of the Wartime Emergency Measures Law promulgated in June in response to the desperate efforts of what was called "scorched-earth resistance." By the Imperial Ordinance empowered by this Emergency Law, the final wartime revision was effected in the taxation law. This revision, aimed at further simplification of the tax system in order to deal with the economic disorder in the country, and called for the temporary suspension of the special tax on interest and dividends and seven other taxes which required complex procedures, despite their being small revenue producers. Another feature of the revision was a novel idea of assessment on estimates for certain income taxes: in order to absorb the surplus purchasing power of the "war rich" and to attain a fair and just impost, the classified income tax for Class A and B enterprises, and the estate tax, business tax, and extraordinary profit tax were imposed on estimates of the current year's income, provided that the income exceeded 50 percent of the actual record of the preceding year.

Taxes suspended by the emergency measures included the special tax on bonds in foreign currency, building tax, securities transfer tax, electricity and gas tax, advertisement tax, horse-racing tax, and stamp tax. The resultant decrease in treasury receipts was estimated at 40 million yen for fiscal 1945 and at 69 million yen for a normal year.

TABLE 17

CLASSIFICATION OF EXPENDITURES OF THE GENERAL ACCOUNT AND THE SPECIAL ACCOUNT FOR EXTRAORDINARY WAR EXPENSES

(In thousand yen)

General Account	*1940–41*	*1944–45*
Imperial household	4,500	4,500
Ministry of Foreign Affairs	66,779	44,955
Ministry of Home Affairs	524,059	2,175,089
Ministry of Finance	1,718,388	10,958,745
Ministry of Justice	57,889	87,067
Ministry of Education	194,954	588,528
Ministry of Agriculture and Forestry	333,568	....
Ministry of Industry and Commerce	147,745	....
Ministry of Agriculture and Commerce	....	2,077,075
Ministry of Communication	381,228	....
Ministry of Transportation and Communication	....	781,603
Ministry of Overseas Affairs	53,923	....
Ministry of Welfare	150,994	585,452
Ministry of War	1,192,469	728
Ministry of Navy	1,033,711	1,145
Ministry of Great East Asia	....	616,883
Ministry of Munition	....	1,950,172
Special Account		
Net amount of special account for extraordinary war expense	5,121,793	66,287,058
Total	10,982,000	86,159,000

IV. *Tax Reforms after World War II*

WITH the end of hostilities, war expenditures became unnecessary, but there emerged new expenditures for the Allied occupation and the rehabilitation of ruined land and productive power. Funds were also needed to subsidize the low-price policy set up to maintain a minimum living standard of the people. All this scarcely permitted the contraction of public finance. Not only that, inflation, which had been suppressed during the war, broke out immediately afterward, and its rapid progress created a new problem for public finance. These difficulties, working together with the economic disorder and the decline in morale caused by the defeat in war, fostered inefficient tax administration and invited tax evasion.

The postwar tax reforms were characterized by two features: an adjustment of taxation to accelerating inflation; and the democratization of the system of taxation in harmony with the economic democratization resulting from a critical evaluation of the old Japanese social structure which had been responsible for bringing on the war. The first feature, the adjustment to inflation, involved two phases: the first was to take into account the wide discrepancy between the nominal value and the real value of commodities caused by inflation; the second was the formulation of a taxation system that would combat inflation itself. The second feature, democratization, also had two aspects. One was the necessity to respect the taxpayer's personal rights and ensure his voluntary cooperation. The other was recognition of the inherent equality of men which is inconsistent with discrimination between rich and poor or on the grounds of advantages or disadvantages created by war or other accidental causes. As inflation developed, each of these ideas was pushed to the fore in turn, to suit the immediate dilemma. With currency stability in sight, the second stage of the postwar period approached, as the people gradually became composed enough to think of the replenishment of their living and the recovery of production. Table 18 illustrates postwar economic conditions in regard to currency and

TABLE 18

ECONOMIC INDICES AFTER THE WAR, 1946–1951

Date	*Cash and Deposit Currency*[a] *(In million yen)*	*Index of Industrial Activity*[b] *(1932–36 average = 100)*	*Production Index for Textile Industry*[b] *(1932–36 average = 100)*	*Tokyo Black Market and Free Market Index, Consumer Goods*[c] *(Sept. 1945 = 100)*	*Consumer's Price Index, Tokyo*[d] *(1948 = 100)*	*Laborer Wage Index*[e] *(1948 = 100)*
1946						
June	57,284	50.5	8.0	201		
Dec.	110,296	54.5	18.6	222	30.1	
1947						
June	156,758	61.7	17.9	419	59.6	
Dec.	250,387	57.5	12.8	558	80.4	
1948						
June	267,510	71.9	17.7	760	111.3	90.0
Dec.	416,562	85.7	20.6	769	124.6	170.2
1949						
June	359,462	94.8	23.2	801	138.9	165.7
Dec.	427,987	100.5	27.7	655	130.9	210.2
1950						
June	375,059	109.6	39.8	480	118.2	194.3
Dec.	529,263	134.0	49.1	580	127.0	281.2
1951						
June	518,529	152.4	51.6	638	140.5	260.6
Dec.	667,541	154.4	59.1	638	152.3	412.1

[a] The Bank of Japan. [b] ESS, GHQ. [c] Statistics Department, the Bank of Japan.
[d] Statistics Bureau, Prime Minister's Office.
[e] "Monthly Labor Survey" by the Ministry of Labor.

commodities and provides a clear background for taxation reforms after the war.

During this period, a matter of foremost importance was the erection of a fundamental policy to wipe out the totalitarian structure once and for all and, by starting from the bottom of the local autonomous governments, to let democracy penetrate into every area of society. Efforts were concentrated in strengthening the local taxation system which had been badly neglected during the war. Ever since Japan was first modernized in the beginning of the Meiji Era (1868-1912), the policy of centralization had been dominant, even in local government and its taxation system. For this reason, the reforms adopted over a period of several years after the war were so significant as to remind us of the Copernican theory. Especially striking was the change in the relationship between the national and local taxation systems.

REVISION OF MARCH, 1946

The atomic bomb dropped on Hiroshima shocked the whole of Japan. The policy of "scorched-earth resistance" was abandoned and unconditional surrender ensued on August 15, 1945. This was followed by the Allied occupation of Japan, and all policies were carried out in conformity with the provisions laid down in the Potsdam Declaration. In addition to the loss of territory, the war destroyed a quarter of Japan's national wealth, and the capital accumulated during the previous thirty to forty years was washed away. Not only was the productivity of the agricultural land curtailed because of abusive cultivation for many years in the past, but also any industrial productive power that was left undamaged was of no use until it could be converted for peacetime industry. Transportation and communication facilities had also been torn to pieces, with little prospect of restoration within a foreseeable time. The mental apathy and dejection of the people helped reduce the economic foundation to complete disorder. Immediately before the end of the war government funds were released in large quantities to settle such national debts as the unpaid accounts of munitions, indemnities for war-devastated plants, and soon this, working together with the social unrest created by surrender, caused a sharp advance in prices. To make the situation worse, latent purchasing power, which had been forcibly restricted so long, even for the necessities of life, was now let loose as the people rushed to withdraw their bank deposits, a sum estimated at 170,000 million yen. When the restriction on consumption was lifted, mounting commodity prices induced the conversion of money into goods; withdrawals of savings began, and inflation was on the march.

Simultaneously with the publication of a draft of the new Constitution early in 1946, affirming the principle of the sovereignty of the people, public finance was also affected. Directives that limited government disbursements financed by debts and restricted investments by the Deposit Bureau or the Postal Life Insurance were issued and enforced by the Occupation Forces. About that time, it was rumored that the government was contemplating a measure to check inflation by levying a corporation property tax, an individual capital levy, a tax on increase of property held by individuals, and a corporation war profits tax. The sensitive public reacted to the rumor and in anticipation of government action an inevitable run on the banks followed. To meet the situation and to stall inflation a drastic measure was taken in February that froze deposits and converted banknotes into new ones; this was followed in March by a series of steps toward economic stabilization, including policies with regard to prices and emergency employment.

In the taxation system, in accordance with the official price structure set by the policy above referred to, it was necessary to revise the exemptions which had been based upon the former prices or wages. From March to May, revisions were made in the income tax, the business tax, the amusement, eating and drinking tax, the admissions tax, the special admissions tax, the special acts tax, and the commodity tax. More specifically, in the category of classified income tax, the basic exemption allowable for incomes from Class A and B business enterprises was raised to 1,200 yen, that of Class A earned income to 2,400 yen, the tax deduction for family dependents to 72 yen per person, and the exemption limit of the aggregate income tax was raised to 10,000 yen. These were major changes, and similar steps were taken for other taxes. This was the first reduction of tax attempted since the war period. The reduction of revenue was estimated at 218 million yen.

REVISION OF SEPTEMBER, 1946

Contrary to expectation, commodity prices did not fall after the adoption of these emergency measures, and daily necessities disappeared from markets immediately upon resumption of distribution controls. An acute shortage of food caused delays in the distribution of food rations throughout the nation, and nation-wide mass demonstrations broke out. In the meantime, it became apparent that the stagnancy of production was gradually causing a reduction of supplies. The black market flourished, not only in foodstuffs but also in all kinds of commodities, necessitating frequent revisions in official commodity prices; and the price structure, so elaborately prepared for stabilization in March, collapsed in less than half a year. Not only that, withdrawal of deposits continued to the maximum limits allowable. Although extraordinary war expenditures came to an end, disbursements for the repatriation of Japanese nationals from abroad and for the Allied military occupation emerged as new burdens. In addition, a rise in the personnel and material costs due to inflation forced the government once again to increase national revenue and strengthen public finance. The revision was thus made effective from September. Led by the classified income tax, direct taxes were markedly raised, including the corporation tax, the special corporation tax, the land tax, the house tax, and the business tax. In indirect taxes, such specific items as the liquor tax and the soft drinks tax were also considerably advanced; others were the sugar excise, the textile excise, a part of the commodity tax, the mine-lot tax, the registration tax, the playing-sets tax, the hunting license tax, the securities transfer tax, the horse racing tax, and the reinstated stamp tax. The price of cigarettes under government monopoly had already risen in advance of the revision.

The greatest structural change was the abolition of the extraordinary profit tax, which had long served as an excess profit tax. Now the corporation tax absorbed the corporation extraordinary profit tax and, in a similar manner, the individual extraordinary profit tax was merged with the income tax. The corporation income was divided into ordinary income and excess income, the former being taxed by simple proportional rates and the latter by progressive rates.

In accordance with the conception of equalizing individual wealth in the postwar period, tax rates on property were, generally speaking, heavily increased. Likewise, the classified income tax was so framed that rate on income from property was higher than that on other incomes. Capital gains from real property became taxable and rates on the estate tax for property of high value were raised sharply. Of the eight items of taxes suspended by the Wartime Emergency Measures Law, three (the securities transfer tax, the horse-racing tax, and the stamp tax) were now revived, but five other items (the special tax on dividends and interest, the special tax on bonds in foreign currency, the building tax, the electricity and gas tax, the advertisement tax, and the special acts tax) were abolished in order to maintain the simplification of the taxation system. To rationalize taxation, the textile excise and the commodity tax on textiles and their products were combined into one. While a part of the commodity tax was either exempted or reduced, some Class A commodity taxes were transferred from the retailer to the manufacturer. Exemption limits were raised for the estate tax and amusement, eating and drinking tax, for which no adjustment had been made in the previous revision. The title of the Emergency Taxation Measures Law was changed to the Special Taxation Measures Law, and the contents were renovated, while other laws were abolished, including wartime special laws and others adjusting domestic and foreign relations (such as the law concerning exemption or deduction of national taxes on war-damaged property and that concerning the prevention of double taxation in Japan and Manchuria).

In the meantime, local finance presented a markedly different aspect. Throughout the war period, the financial structure had been rigidly centralized with little consideration given to the local finance; consequently, all local works were virtually suspended. No sooner had the war terminated than local administrations were faced with the necessity of a huge budget for reconstruction and repair. An immediate solution had to be found in order to increase the wages of the local government personnel made necessary by the accelerated inflation. Another difficulty in tax-bearing capacity arose from the fact that the relative financial position of cities and rural communities had now been reversed. The concentrated bombardment of cities had left the inhabitants impoverished, thereby creating an imbalance in wealth between cities (especially war-damaged cities) and rural communities, and at the same time upsetting the equity in tax-bearing capacity between the two.

In order to secure and adjust sources of local revenue, the Local Tax Law and a part of the Local Apportionment Tax Law were revised to raise the rates of surtax on the land and house taxes and the business tax. At the same time, the city, town, and village inhabitant taxes were increased, and taxation over the legal limits was recognized. As a new addition to the local taxation structure, an inhabitant tax was granted to prefectures, with a view to fostering the spirit of local autonomy among the people by making them share the burden of prefectural finance through a direct personal tax. Another innovation was the power granted to prefectural governments to charge extra-legal independent taxes. The grant of these powers, which had already been given to cities, towns, and villages, was intended to ensure flexibility of prefectural finance.

EXTRAORDINARY TAXES OF SEPTEMBER AND DECEMBER, 1946

Reference has already been made to the draft of four new taxes, including the capital levy, which were announced in January to curb inflation. These measures were intended: 1) to remove the causes of inflation once and for all by canceling government obligations in respect to such fictitious capital as accumulated war bonds or government debts to munition factories already destroyed or lost during the war; 2) to equalize wealth; and 3) to reconstruct national finance. Application of these measures was delayed by criticism from various quarters that they were too radical and too extensive in scale.. But despite the fact that the emergency measures effected in March had not produced the desired results, and that the currency issue in September exceeded even the peak figure reached immediately before the adoption of the emergency measures, the government was forced to resort to the drastic step of canceling all war indemnities and eliminating the fictitious capital connected therewith. As the first step, the frozen deposits were divided into first class and second class by revising the Emergency Financial Measures Ordinance in August, and the assets and liabilities of financial institutions and other corporations which might be affected by the cancellation of war indemnities were separated by the Emergency Accounting Measures Law into old and new accounts, the former representing war indemnities accounts and the latter regular accounts.

By the War Indemnities Special Tax of October, a 100 percent tax was levied on the amount of claims for war indemnities or on the amounts already paid for such claims. The self-assessment system was adopted for payment of these taxes. The war indemnity claims terminated by the measure were estimated at 66,955 million yen, and the actual tax revenue therefrom was 16,413 million yen (of which 12,630 million yen was to be collected during fiscal 1946).

With the cancellation of war indemnities disposed of, the corporation war profit tax and the corporation property tax were abandoned first and later the individual increased-property tax. Thus, of the new tax plan announced in January, only the capital levy for individuals was left, and this was so altered later that the estimated revenue was reduced by half to 43,500 million yen; its appropriation, accordingly, was modified to cover the deficit of revenue during the fiscal year, instead of redeeming government bonds as originally contemplated.

The basis of the capital levy was fixed as the value of an individual's property at the time specified, less liabilities, allowing an exemption limit of 100,000 yen; the steeply progressive tax rates ranged from 25 percent up to 90 percent. The tax was paid by a self-assessment system computed on the following basis: for deposits and government bonds, the value appraised by the Emergency Property Investigation Ordinance issued in February, together with the Emergency Financial Measures Ordinance; for real property, the rental value multiplied by certain formulated rates; and for stocks and so on, the rate was set on the value of every type on the basis of quotations during a certain period.

The tax on increase in income differed completely from the foregoing two taxes. It was intended, first of all, to provide immediate revenue to meet increasing disbursements for the Allied occupation and other expenses. Secondly, since the income tax law was expected to be so revised in 1947 as to adopt the self-assessment system based on the income during the current year (instead of the preceding year as hithertofore), it was feared that it might fail to catch the actual income for 1946. Accordingly, this temporary tax was levied on such 1946 income as might markedly exceed that of the preceding year. The measure was put in force in December.

Income subject to the increased-income tax were classified into: 1) income from real properties and from Class A and Class B business enterprises; 2) forestry income; and 3) capital gains from the transfer of real estate and other transaction. For the first group, progressive rates ranging from 30 percent to 90 percent were applied to the excess of income over that of the preceding year, after deducting the basic exemption. For the second group, the rates were from 20 percent to 60 percent and for the third, from 25 percent to 65 percent, all at progressive rates. In each case, the tax was imposed on the amount assessed by the government on the basis declared by the taxpayer. The revenue through this channel was estimated at 4,534 million yen.

REVISION OF APRIL, 1947

By the promulgation of an epoch-making Constitution in November, 1946, the foundation of democratic Japan was firmly established, but the progress of national recovery was far from reassuring. In industrial fields, the increase in production, which had been painfully slow, came to a standstill after October, 1946; stocks were critically depleted, causing a further advance in commodity prices and the cost of living. The purge, which was extended to economic and press circles, advanced the democratization of the country, but, on the other hand, labor offensives were intensified more than ever before, finally developing to the threat of a nation-wide walkout scheduled for February 1, 1947. The disaster was fortunately averted by General MacArthur's directive issued on the eve of the strike. In view of all this, the government planned a priority production system for such essential commodities as coal, iron, and steel; in the meantime severe steps were taken to suppress the black-market transactions which were at the root of the economic disorder. In order to reinforce it, attempts were made to control the allocation of certain production materials and the distribution of specified commodities. Intensification of these controls was of no avail; instead, underground black markets spread, and no improvement was seen in the issue of currency or in the level of production.

Despite a marked decrease in real national income due to inflation and the impasse of production, national expenditures did not recede in the presence of many problems of postwar rehabilitation. Whatever changes and revisions were made, the taxation system then in force was after all a modified form of the wartime system; if revenues were to be stabilized under the new democratized postwar social conditions, a revolutionary reform of the taxation system was imperative. The tax revision of 1947 was made in response to this demand. Its purpose was to tighten the income tax as the nucleus of the taxation structure, to extend the self-assessment system to principal taxes, and to adjust the exemption limits to the depreciated currency. The revision also aimed at adjusting the national and local systems to provide the foundation for local financial autonomy. A summary of the revisions is given below.

The income tax. The distinction between the classified income tax and the aggregate income tax was discontinued, and all incomes were consolidated into one item, on which progressive rates were applied. Tax was levied on income from the current year, and not for the preceding year as in the past. It was payable four times a year on three provisional declarations based on estimates made in the current year, and the final adjustment payment was to be made with the final return based on the actual annual income at the end of the fiscal year. The basic exemption was fixed at 4,800 yen; the deduction for earned income was raised to 20 percent, and the dependency credit to 240 yen per person respectively, the tax rates ranging from 20 percent up to 75 percent at progressive rates. Tax on earned incomes, dividends, interest, and so on was collected at the source, to be adjusted at the time of the final return. A special period of declaration was provided for the farmer, whose income is concentrated in harvest season.

The corporation and special corporation taxes. The tax rates for excess incomes and capital were revised, and the self-assessment system was extended to include all corporations, declaration to be made within two months after the conclusion of the fiscal business term, when the tax was to be paid. Corporations whose closing accounts could not be completed within the above period or whose fiscal term extended over six months were subject to taxation by an approximate self-assessment. The special corporation tax was similarly treated, except that a declaration was to be made within one month after the conclusion of the fiscal term, and no approximate self-assessment was allowed.

Estate and gift taxes. In line with the revised Inheritance Law of the Civil Code, the distinction between the estate tax of succession to a house and succession to a property was abolished, the system of exemption limit was changed to the basic exemption, abolishing dependency credits. The rates were intensified, and the method of payment was changed to the self-assessment system, allowing payment in kind. In regard to gifts, provisions of the old estate tax law were broadened and the gift tax established as a new tax item. Donors were responsible for payment of tax, and the principle of cumulative computation was adopted for the calculation of the basic exemption and taxable amount. These taxes were paid once a year by self-assessment.

Other national taxes. Liquor (sake) was divided into two classifications, one for family use and the other for business use to be sold in restaurants or bars; the rates were raised and an additional tax was added to the second classification. Rates were increased for the securities transfer tax, the registration tax, the soft drink tax, the sugar excise, the bourse tax, the stamp tax, the playing-sets tax, a part of the commodity tax, the admissions tax, the special admission tax, and the hunting license tax. On the other hand, the textile excise and a part of the commodity tax were reduced. Through these changes, the increase in tax revenue was estimated at 43,137 million yen for 1947 and 40,870 million yen for a normal year. At the same time, raising the prices of monopoly tobacco was expected to produce an increased revenue of 14,994 million yen.

In the past, the mainstay of local revenues was a real estate tax, which had little flexibility in a period of inflation. The local apportionment tax had served to make up deficiencies in local revenue. This system, incidentally, had been one of the characteristics of the development of local autonomy in Japan. However, the fact that the new Constitution guaranteed local autonomy, and that local autonomy was pushed forward as a part of the national democratization program, required a fundamental re-examination of the local system. It was, therefore, decided to transfer to local governments as their independent sources of revenue these items: three taxes (land, house, and business) for which local governments had depended on the central government as refund taxes (returned to place of origin); amusement, eating and drinking taxes, which had been distributive taxes; and the mine-lot tax. Other distributive taxes such as income, corporation, and admissions taxes were left as a means of adjustment.

Cities, towns, and villages were allowed to levy a surtax on the land, house, and business taxes, which were made prefectural independent taxes. The standard rates for these taxes remained substantially the same as before the transfer. But because the rental value of land and houses on which tax amounts were determined had remained unchanged despite the rise in the general price level, exceptions were granted in excess of the standard rates. To facilitate the change in registration of land and houses following the transfer of the real estate tax to local governments, the Land and House registration Ledger Law was enacted, the original ledgers to be kept by the taxation offices and copies by cities, towns, and villages.

The telephone subscription right tax, the automobile and ship acquisition taxes, the railway-line tax, the bath tax, and the admissions tax were also added to independent prefectural taxes. As independent taxes of cities, towns, and villages, the boat acquisition tax and the advertisement tax were added to legal taxes. The inhabitant tax was raised for prefectures and cities, towns, and villages. The tax rate for the city-planning tax was unified, and the water-utilization tax was enlarged to include the irrigation and land-reclaim tax.

REVISION OF DECEMBER, 1947

The super-priority production policy had so far failed to bring about the expected result, the increase of currency issue continued unabated, delays in the deliveries of food rations again started to appear, and there was no sign of an end to the vicious cycle of rising commodity prices and wages. The government tried to adjust currency circulation, and, to reach a new, stable level for wages, altered the price structure by a big upward swing of official commodity prices in July. The attempt to stabilize official commodity prices failed again. To make the stiuation worse, such a large increase in official prices naturally affected the budget, requiring a supplementary budget, and taxes again had to be revised despite the over-all revision that had been made that same year; this time it was a partial revision, except for the introduction of a special tax on those who suffered no loss of income or property through the war.

A raise in the deduction for earned income and dependency credit in proportion with advance of prices was indicated. It was also intended that the tax burden of the general masses and of the group grown newly rich in blackmarket operation would be equalized by collecting a particularly heavy tax from the latter. Moreover, the sales of liquor for business use were made free, provided that the tax be raised both in ordinary rate and additional rate. The revision also included a rate increase for the corporation tax, the registration tax, the soft drink tax, a part of the commodity tax, the admissions tax, the special admissions tax, the playing-sets tax, the stamp tax, and the hunting license tax.

The special tax on those who suffered no financial loss through the war consisted of the non-damaged houses tax and the non-war-sufferers tax, collectible only once. In regard to the first tax, about three times the rental value of houses was levied on the owners of houses standing at the end of the war. For the second, the same percentage of rental value was levied on houses where non-war-sufferers resided at the time the tax was imposed. The self-assessment system was adopted for this tax, both for corporations and individuals.

REVISION OF JULY, 1948

Democratization of Japan's economy reached a climax in 1947 by the enforcement of the Anti-Monopoly Law and the Excess Economic Power Deconcentration Law. In 1948, there appeared signs, in the occupation policy, of encouraging the economic independence of Japan, as witnessed in the reports prepared by the Strike and Draper mission. In the meantime, the priority production system began to show its effect gradually, and the release of large funds by the Reconstruction Finance Bank, established in the latter half of 1946, also contributed to a slow but steady revival of the production level.

Strenuous efforts were made by the government, supported by GHQ, in early 1948 to ensure tax collection. This resulted in a good recovery of treasury funds from the public in the fourth quarter of fiscal 1947, contracting currency issue for the first time since the enforcement of the Financial Emergency Measures Ordinance, and there were devoutly welcomed signs of a lull in the inflationary trend. However, sharply swollen commodity prices and wages since 1947, and expenditures relative to the occupation and various subsidies, necessitated far larger Treasury funds than in the previous years, and demanded a greater tax revenue. In planning a revision, however, it was found necessary to adjust and rationalize the tax burden to correct a possibly unfair distribution.

Increases were made in the liquor tax, the soft drinks tax, the sugar excise, a part of the commodity tax, the registration tax, the playing-sets tax, and the stamp tax, all of which were on a specific or a fixed amount basis, together with the securities transfer tax and the transaction tax. The travel tax was moved from the mileage basis to the ad valorem category.

The rates and the basic exemption of the income tax, as well as the exemption limit of the estate tax, were revised. The special corporation tax became a part of the corporation tax, and at the same time, measures were taken to lessen the tax burden of corporations, thereby to promote industry on the one hand and to induce foreign investments on the other. The promulgation of a new horse racing law reduced the horse racing tax to almost nil. To make partial restitution for the deficiency in the income tax and the corporation tax under the revision, the transaction tax (sales tax) was newly instituted. Meanwhile, some taxes (such as the hunting license and the admissions taxes) were transferred to local entities from the central government to strengthen the independence of the local taxation system. This series of revisions resulted in a drop of 28,649 million yen in the national tax revenues.

Details of the revised income tax were as follows: 1) upping of the basic exemption to 15,000 yen, the dependency credit to 1,800 yen, and maximum exemption of earned incomes to 25 percent; 2) revision of progressive rates and bracket scales, leaving the lowest taxable point untouched. These measures resulted in a drastic cut in the income tax. In addition, a special credit for the income tax on dividends was permitted to an extent of 15 percent of dividends received from corporations. Also, it was arranged to apply the same rate for foreign corporations and individuals as for Japanese corporations and individuals.

Revisions relative to the corporation tax were: 1) abrogation of the tax on capital; 2) reduction of the rate of tax on excess-incomes; 3) reduction of the rates for small corporations; 4) lowering the rates on ordinary incomes of foreign corporations to the level of domestic corporations; and 5) abolition of the special corporation tax by incorporating special corporations into ordinary corporations, instead of treating them separately under separate regulations.

The newly instituted transaction tax was a "circulation" tax imposed on business transactions. It had the advantage of being elastic in collection in inflation periods. Trade transactions were subject to the tax at the rate of one percent of the amount involved. The payment was made with appropriate revenue stamps or certificates, with the exception of payment in cash for some small transactions of less than 50 yen or transactions for which the use of stamps or certificates was difficult or impracticable. Payers of the tax were under obligation to declare quarterly to the tax office the amount of transactions and tax during the period.

As local autonomy progressed, the necessity for local independence was stressed and the Local Finance Law was enacted to implement the Local Autonomy Law. Accordingly, this latest revision was so framed as to make local taxes independent of national taxes and to minimize supervision of the central government over local finance. The Ministry of Home Affairs, which had been handling the local administration for many years, was dissolved at the end of 1947 and the Local Finance Commission was created to take over these duties.

The actual increase in revenue under the revision of 1947 was again found insufficient and too inflexible to keep pace with inflation, and it was necessary to make a fresh revision of local taxes. Revenues from business taxes and the amusement tax, which had been transferred to local revenues, did not come up to expectations because business taxes were to be collected on the basis of net profit for the previous year and the amusement tax was impaired by the Ordinance of July 5, 1947, which banned amusement in restaurants.

The surtax system was done away with and independent tax sources were given to local governments by the revision of 1947. The same principle was pursued in effecting the new revision. The admissions tax and the hunting license tax were transferred to local governments. Several new taxes were added to the list of independent taxes, including the special income tax, the mine product tax, the electricity and gas tax, the liquor consumption tax, the timber trade tax, the domestic employee tax, and the spare-room house tax. At the same time, a number of taxes were expanded in scope or upped in rates. They were the prefectural inhabitant's tax, the land tax, the house tax, the enterprise tax, the mine-lot tax, the acquisition of real property tax, the amusement, eating and drinking tax (renamed), the city, town, or village inhabitant's tax, the service-girl tax (formerly known as the "geisha girl tax," renamed after being transferred from prefectural to municipal governments), the bicycle tax, the boat tax, and the safe tax.

Concurrently with the rise in rates, a system of the standard tax rate, inclusive of municipal surtaxes, was instituted to be applied to principal taxes, such as the inhabitant's tax, the amusements tax, and the three profit taxes. Authorization by the supervisory office of the central government for levying excess taxes within the limit of the standard rates was made unnecessary. The system of authorization by the supervisory office for the institution or alteration of extra independent taxes which were not legally recognized was also withdrawn, with the exception of special cases requiring the submission of reports to the superior office. These were entirely novel ideas and particularly noteworthy as a turning point in the history of the local taxation system in view of the fact that local finance had been at the mercy of the central government ever since the institution of the taxation system in Japan far back in the Meiji Era (1868-1912).

New independent taxes. The mine product tax had existed as a national tax until 1939. It was canceled but was revived as a local tax in the revision of 1948. The tax was imposed on mining and collection of minerals, inclusive of alluvial, on their prices at the rate of 4/1000 for prefectural governments and 6/1000 for municipal governments as a surtax. This was a taxation on an external standard (French method).

The electricity and gas tax was levied during the war as a national tax. Its content was similar in the revived form, the rate being 10 percent, including a surtax. Some prefectures retained these taxes as independent taxes (not legally recognized) up to their revival in the 1948 revision, even after they had been abolished as national taxes.

The timber trade tax was imposed on deliveries of raw timber on the basis of price or measurement. In the case of a price basis the rate was 6 percent including a surtax. The tax had existed in many localities as an independent tax, but had not been legally recognized.

The liquor consumption tax was paid by sake consumers at the rate of 2.5 percent of its retail price. As explained previously, the liquor tax and tobacco monopoly revenue had been regarded as the most sensitive and elastic of all the national taxes during inflation. As a local revenue source, too, this tax, together with the admissions tax, which also was transferred to local entities under the 1948 revision, was considered as having the most elastic character capable of meeting inflation. The rate of the admissions tax was fixed at 150 percent inclusive of a surtax. (The rate of the special admissions tax, 60 percent, was combined with the admissions tax.) The hunting license tax, which had previously been in existence under the name of hunters tax, was also imposed.

The domestic employee tax, a municipal tax, was levied on employers of one or more domestic servants.

A municipal tax, called the spare-room house tax, was imposed on spare-rooms or vacant houses as provided for in the Housing Emergency Measure Ordinance enforced in Tokyo and other war-damaged municipalities.

The dog and electric fan taxes, which formerly belonged to municipalities, were deleted from the category of legal independent taxes because of the small revenues therefrom.

By the Law No. 111, July 7, 1948, the Local Distribution Tax Law was enacted in place of the Local Apportionment Tax Law. As a result, the refund tax system (100 percent return of revenue by national government to locality of origin) was abolished and the distributive tax system alone remained.

REVISION OF APRIL, 1949

The month of July, 1948, saw the revision of the taxation system as explained in the previous section and also the passage of the delayed budget for fiscal 1948. The same month also witnessed a revision in the price structure in an attempt to bring official prices closer to black-market prices. Further, the government announced a ten-point economic policy to stabilize the currency. However, the effect upon wages caused by the upward price revision was far greater than anticipated by the government. Disbursements of Treasury funds, which had been withheld pending Diet approval of the budget, were started.

All these factors pointed to currency expansion and the revival of the inflationary trend. The trend was not reversed until the government enunciated a series of strong and decisive policies in the latter part of 1948 (including a three-point principle for enterprises and a nine-point principle for economy), which culminated in the formulation of a super-balanced budget for 1949. This was prepared in accordance with the so-called Dodge Line Policy laid down by Mr. Joseph M. Dodge, who came to Japan in February, 1949.

The Dodge Line Policy insisted that the cause and the cure of inflation were to be found in public finance. Expenditures should be cut to the minimum to permit a "super-balanced budget." All loans from the Reconstruction Finance Bank should be suspended. In order to restore Japan's economy to normal status and push ahead the principle of a free economy, the establishment of a single exchange rate in place of bilateral rates was recommended.

By the rationalization of government finance thus contemplated, the year's budget, despite a large fund provided for national debt retirement, allowed a margin to be applied to some tax reduction, and this led to a revision in corporation taxes and others. Prior to this, early in January, 1949, the Taxation System Deliberative Council was organized to investigate the long-pending issue of the public tax burden, which had been regarded as too heavy in proportion to national income. The Council immediately started deliberations on the possibility of lightening the tax burden and also on a new taxation system capable of meeting recent changes in economic conditions.

Two factors intervened: a budget margin that might have been used for tax reduction was withheld for retirement of national debts, as provided for in the Dodge Line budget; and it was reported that Dr. Carl S. Shoup would shortly visit Japan to make a thorough investigation of the taxation system. The Council therefore decided to limit the proposed revision to a transitional adjustment: a partial amendment of the income, corporation, liquor, transactions, sugar, soft drinks, commodity, and stamp taxes, and the introduction of a gasoline tax.

Under the revision, a capital subscription exceeding the face value of corporation stocks was exempted from the corporation tax, the liquor tax on both the rationed sake and the special-priced sake was reduced, while imported sugar was made tax-free from the sugar excise. The system of paying the transaction tax in the form of stamps was repealed. The new gasoline tax was levied on receipt of gasoline from a refinery or bonded area on the assessment standard of its price at the rate of 100 percent. The tax was estimated to yield some 4,052 million yen.

As a result of the retrenchment policy in public finance, the rate of the distributive tax, which had been guaranteed to local entities in the revision of the previous year, was cut down. This forced local governments to raise the tax rates in their jurisdictions to meet expanding local finance. With the exception of a reduction of the admissions tax, an all-round raise was effected in the inhabitant's tax, the real property tax, the mine-lot tax, and the hunting license tax. To facilitate collection, a system of payment of the admissions tax with certificates was adopted, and the method of computing the assessment of the enterprise tax was partly simplified. Up to that time, the surtax for city planning, which fell under the category of the special purpose tax, had been imposed on almost all independent taxes; now it was limited to four: land, house, enterprise, and special income. Actually, however, the revision in this respect had no particular effect on revenue, as these taxes formed the major part of local revenue. A creditable aspect was that the change helped to consolidate the local taxation structure to a great extent. Another feature was an intensification of the tax collection method by local bodies, by which local tax officials were given the same authority that national tax collectors possessed under the law concerning evasion of national taxes.

The transfer of the admissions tax made some municipalities extremely prosperous. To rectify the imbalance, prefectures were authorized to restrict the rate of the admissions tax in localities enjoying too much revenue from this source and to levy an extra prefectural tax equivalent to the amount thus reduced. At the same time, the prefectures were empowered to ban or restrict the imposition of a surtax on their extralegal independent taxes. These steps were taken in an attempt to rationalize the distribution of revenue sources among local entities.

DEVELOPMENT OF THE TAXATION SYSTEM, 1940 TO 1950

Japan's taxation system underwent a drastic reform in 1950 as a result of a scrutiny made by the Shoup Mission. The mission was sent over to Japan at the request of the Supreme Commander of the Allied Forces. Headed by Dr. Shoup, it consisted of seven members as follows: Carl S. Shoup, Graduate School of Business and Graduate Faculty of Political Science, Columbia University; Howard R. Bowen, College of Commerce and Business Administration, University of Illinois; Jerome B. Cohen, Department of Economics, College of the City of New York; Rolland F. Hatfield, Director of Tax Research, Department of Taxation, St. Paul, Minnesota; Stanley S. Surrey, School of Jurisprudence, University of California, Berkeley, Calif.; William Vickrey, Graduate Faculty of Political Science, Columbia University; William C. Warren, School of Law, Columbia University.

At the recommendation of the mission, the Japanese government

TABLE 19

MAJOR CHANGES IN INTERRELATION BETWEEN NATIONAL AND LOCAL TAXATION, 1940–1950

	1940	*1947*	*1948*	*1950*
National government	National tax (Independent tax)	National tax (Independent tax)	National tax (Independent tax)	National tax (Independent tax)
	Local apportionment tax (apportioned to local governments)	Local apportionment tax (apportioned to local governments)	Local distributive tax (distributed to local governments, a fixed rate of income and corporation taxes)	Local Finance Equalization grants (granted to local governments, no specified revenue sources)
	Refund tax (all of land, house, and business taxes are returned to the place of collection)	Distributive tax (a fixed rate of income, corporation, and admission taxes)		
	Distributive tax (a fixed rate of income, corporation, amusements, eating and drinking, and admission taxes)			
Prefectures	Prefectural tax	Prefectural tax (Independent tax)	Prefectural tax (Independent tax)	Prefectural (Independent tax)
	Surtax on the national tax			
	Independent tax			
	Local apportionment tax (received from the national government)	Local apportionment tax (received from national government)		Local Finance Equalization grants (received from national government)
	Refund tax			
	Distributive tax	Distributive tax	Distributive tax (received from national government)	
Municipalities	Municipal tax	Municipal tax	Municipal tax	Municipal tax (Independent tax)
	Surtax	Surtax on the prefectural tax	Surtax on the prefectural tax	
	Surtax on the national tax			
	Surtax on the prefectural tax			
	Independent tax	Independent tax	Independent tax	
	Local apportionment tax (received from the national government)	Local apportionment tax (received from national government)	Distributive tax (received from national government)	Local Finance Equalization grants (received from central government)
	Distributive tax	Distributive tax		

made a revolutionary reform of the taxation system. In effecting the reform, the tax burden of the Japanese people was studied in an international setting and an overall reduction was carried out, in careful coordination with the Dodge Line Policy designed to promote the accumulation of capital so badly needed for rehabilitation.

Ever since the early days of the Meiji Era, Japan's taxation system had developed under the strong influence of Continental Law. If its peak could be regarded as having been reached in 1940, its outstanding characteristic was the priority of the national tax system. With the exception of a few independent taxes, local governments were only allowed to impose a surtax—even with respect to taxes that might be considered primarily local taxes, relying on the national government for considerable financial assistance in the form of the local apportionment tax.

The 1950 reform, however, was definitely patterned after Anglo-American law. A clear-cut division was made in revenue sources between the national government and local governments, making it possible to collect taxes independently. The changes made in this period in the national and local taxation structure were so great that one is apt to lose sight of their real meaning. Table 19 summarizes the major changes in the fiscal relationship between the national government and local governments, from 1940 to 1950.

V. *The Shoup Mission Recommendations*

THE recommendations of Dr. Shoup's Mission on Japan's taxation system deserves a full chapter. When a brief summary was made public on August 26, 1949, there was an impression that the recommendations were not of a drastic enough character, and not until the full text of the four volumes was made public (two on September 15 and two on October 3) was it realized that this would create a revolution in the Japanese taxation system and lay a new foundation for the whole system of tax administration.

LOCAL TAX SYSTEM

First, in the Shoup recommendations, great stress is put on decentralization.

Abolition of the surtax system. Japan's taxation system before the war was highly centralized, and nearly all prefectural taxes and municipal taxes were surtaxes levied on national taxes. After the war, the national surtax system was discontinued altogether and prefectural taxes and prefectural surtaxes took its place. Municipal taxes, upon which local autonomy rested, depended on prefectures in a form of prefectural surtaxes.

However, in both prefectural and municipal taxation, the enterprise taxes were levied on assessments which had been determined by the national tax office for the purpose of levying a national income tax on individual enterprise income or a national corporation tax on a corporation's ordinary income. In other words, they were not assessed independently; instead, the assessments made by the national tax office were applied, unchanged, to local enterprise taxes.

The land and house taxes were also assessed on the rental values fixed at the national tax office. In substance, although the national surtaxes had technically been repealed, local taxes were actually dependent on the assessments made at the national office. The Shoup recommendations made a fundamental reform in this respect.

Reduction in groups of municipal and prefectural taxes. Thirty-one groups of municipal taxes were reduced to eleven, and twenty-one groups of prefectural taxes, to nine. Not only the number of tax groups was thus greatly reduced, but, on a priority principle, three important taxes, the value-added tax, the admissions tax, and the amusement, eating and drinking tax, were elevated to such a position that they would produce almost all prefectural expenditures. Similarly, the inhabitant's tax (local income tax) and the municipal property tax (real estate tax) were made the principal taxes for municipal budgets.

Reduction in national taxes and increase in local taxes. It was recommended that national taxes be reduced by 60 billion yen and that an increase of 40 billion yen be made in local taxes, comprising 39 billion yen in municipal taxes and one billion yen in prefectural taxes. This followed a natural course in the decentralization of Japanese authority to replace the extremely centralized character of ultra-nationalism.

With regard to the tax administration, municipalities were placed foremost, prefectures next, and the national government last, and then to attend only to matters that could not be administered locally. Some amalgamation of prefectures, cities, towns, and villages was thought of, to avoid duplication of administration. In short, the course was set to reduce national taxes and increase local taxes, particularly municipal taxes.

It must be remembered that the great majority of tax administrators served in national offices and very few in local ones. Since the business of the national offices was now considerably reduced and that of the local offices had mushroomed, it was feared that some friction might result. The proposed measures were completely novel to the Japanese, and they had to tackle problems entirely different from any they had faced before. Localization of control was one of the great problems to be thrashed out before the reformed tax system could be successfully enforced.

THE NATIONAL TAX SYSTEM

Repeal of circulation taxes, reduction of consumption taxes, and readjustment of revenue taxes. The framework of the Japanese taxation system, for national as well as local taxes, had been patterned after the Continental European system. It had circulation taxes and consumption taxes in addition to revenue taxes (income, property, and other taxes). Some taxes were collectible on assessments wherein taxpayers might deal directly with tax collectors. The idea of imposing consumption taxes and circulation taxes to a fairly large extent reflected a desire to emphasize those taxes which were collectible indirectly.

Japan's consumption taxes had been fairly well developed and established, but the circulation taxes had been rather ineffective until their recent reinforcement in the shape of a transaction tax. Thus, these three forms of taxes, namely, revenue, consumption and circulation, had been the mainstay of the Japanese tax system.

Dr. Shoup's recommendation was, however, to wipe out circulation taxes altogether, including the securities transfer tax, the transaction tax, the registration tax, and the stamp tax. Locally, the taxes on the acquisition of real estate, bicycles, and carts were also to be repealed This was so drastic a reform that it required a careful study of whether it could be carried out all at once or should be done step by step, depending on its effect on national revenue.

As for consumption taxation, it was recommended that the liquor tax be increased, that the tobacco tax and commodity excises (after some revision) be retained, and that the taxes on sugar, soft drinks, textiles, and travel be repealed.

Of the three pillars which were the mainstay of Japan's tax system as referred to above, the circulation taxes were to be taken away and the consumption taxes to be reduced in application. It was recommended that the taxation system should largely rely upon revenue taxes, that is to say, income and property taxes. It would be a system in which taxes could be collected directly from taxpayers on records or documentary proof. It would follow the British system, rather than the Continental European system under which the tax system was framed.

The old system might be compared with an orchestra in which several instruments such as flutes, drums, strings, and others played their parts, whereas the new system had only one excellent instrument called the revenue tax, especially the income tax.

Such being the case, the pivot of the Japanese taxation system would have to shift from the circulation and the consumption taxes to the revenue tax. Of revenue taxes, the income tax of the modern type was to play a leading role. As in old times when physiocrats regarded the single tax or land tax as the sole revenue producer in national finance, after the reform the income tax would occupy a dominant position in national finance as a revenue source. According to the Mission's recommendation, the income taxes, national and local, would produce 75 percent of the whole taxes ten years hence. It was indeed a great reform.

Since the revenue taxes played the most important part in the national revenue, the property tax, another branch of the revenue taxes, also called for a thorough renovation. The inheritance tax of old days had been the only national property tax in Japan, but now a regular property tax called the net-worth tax was to be added. The net-worth tax was payable regardless of income. There was also the succession tax (an estate tax on any property transferred without compensation). According to the reform, the income tax, although it assumed the same old name, implied many ideals and was quite different in nature from the old one.

The income tax and the readjustment of the corporation tax and property taxation. In regard to the relation between the corporation tax and the income tax, there have been two schools of thought: one is the Anglo-American way of thinking which asserts that since an income of a corporation is that of its shareholders, the income tax should not be imposed on shareholders if there is a tax on corporation income, and, conversely, the tax should not be imposed on a corporation if the shareholders are taxed; the other is the German school which advocates that the income tax should be imposed on a corporation and its shareholders alike.

In Japan, the British system was adopted first and later supplanted by the German system. By the tax reforms enforced in 1920 and 1941, it became completely German. In America, the British system was adopted at first, but, in 1936, in the days of the late President Roosevelt's New Deal, the German system was adopted, although there was strong objection to this measure and voices have since been raised for its revision.

Dr. Shoup boldly recommended the British system for Japan. It was not an adoption of the present American tax system, but an attempt to realize Dr. Shoup's ideal in the Japanese tax system.

We should next consider the relation between property taxation, more particularly the estate and gift taxes, and the income tax. In every country of the world, the rates of the estate tax are generally speaking lower than those of the income tax, for the estate tax is levied on the principal of the property whereas the income tax is imposed on the fruit of the property. However high the rates may be, the income tax will never eat up the principal. The prevailing idea is that if too high a rate is levied on the principal, it will drain capital.

However, according to the Shoup recommendation, the top rate of the accession tax (consisting of the gift tax and the estate tax) was to be as high as 90 percent, whereas the existing top rate of income tax was 80 percent (later reduced to 55 percent). The top rate for the accession tax was later reduced from 90 percent to 70 percent by the revision of 1952. It was seen that the proportion in rates between the tax on transfer of property by gift or a death and the income tax as recommended by the Shoup report was different from what had been practiced in other countries of the world. It was different from the German, French, British, and even the American systems. First set forth in his book published about ten years ago, this was Dr. Shoup's own, original idea, and he then recommended that it be used in the United States, but it has not been put into operation yet.

The idea of the net-worth tax was an annual tax on the net worth of an individual's property. Dr. Vickrey, a member of the Shoup Mission, once wrote a book on the theory of the progressive tax, in which he stated that he would like to see the net-worth tax adopted as a federal tax in America, but he was afraid that it could not materialize for some time to come, as it might be an infringement of the Constitution. Its tryout, therefore, was a unique one.

The value-added tax, recommended as one of local taxes, was also an entirely new tax never adopted before in any country of the world. Although it had been accepted by American academic circles, it had not yet been practiced anywhere.

So much for the general outline of the Shoup recommendations. We turn now to some of the characteristics of the system recommended.

STIMULATION OF PRODUCTION AND DECONCENTRATION OF WEALTH

It seems paradoxical to speak of the stimulation of production and the deconcentration of wealth at the same time. But these were the explicit objectives of the Shoup system. To achieve the first, the maximum rate of the income tax was lowered from 80 percent to 55 percent; the minimum remained at 20 percent. The reasoning was that heavy taxation of high incomes would discourage accumulation and investment of capital. A remark may not be amiss that it is probably very difficult for Americans, whose currency is solidly stabilized and who have only a vague notion of destructive inflation, to grasp the true meaning of depreciated currency. In Japan it was feared that differences of opinion might arise concerning this recommendation. For example, the maximum rate of income tax, 55 percent, was applied to annual incomes over 300,000 yen; the question was whether it was appropriate to apply that same rate to any amount in excess of that sum. (The 300,000 yen limit was raised to 500,000 yen in 1950, to 1,000,000 yen in 1951, and to 2,000,000 yen in 1952.)

In the accession tax, the top rate was applied to the amount above 50 million yen. Before the war, this was certainly a big sum but since commodity prices had risen 200 times, 50 million yen was equlivalent to prewar 250,000 yen. Admitting we had all become poor, it was questionable whether it was justifiable to apply the top rate of the estate tax to the amount equivalent to 250,000 yen in prewar days.

At any rate, it was evident that careful consideration was given to various ways of promoting production; the lightening of the income tax was one, and the readjustment of tax on corporations and individuals to encourage direct investments was another. The writer had no reason whatsoever to dissent with the fundamental principle. It was a matter of degree, a question of how to adjust tax rates to an amount of income designated in terms of an abnormally inflated currency. The lowering of the top rate of the tax from 80 percent to 55 percent was a welcome step.

As to deconcentration of wealth, a heavy tax would be levied on all transfers of property without compensation, whether they were bequeathed by parents or presented by others. While the imposition of a heavy tax on income might not be approved altogether, it was reasonable to impose a heavy tax on properties acquired without compensation. The idea of dissolving the Zaibatsu (family groups of great wealth) and breaking up the concentration of wealth was well embodied in the new plan. A large fortune could be amassed in one generation, but the second generation could not inherit it intact. Removal of excessive concentration of wealth was one of the objectives set forth in the terms of surrender. But here again the question of degree was open to discussion, and it was no easy matter to decide what should be considered excessive.

PENETRATION OF INDIVIDUALISM

Throughout the newly recommended accession tax and the income tax, there could be found a degree of penetration of individualism, incorporated in a tax law, that can scarcely be matched in the tax laws of any other country. In both taxes, conjugal relations were considered, but parental relations were almost ignored. Especially in the accession tax, no distinction was recognized among gifts of any kind, whether they came from parents, relatives, or others, or whether the donor was dead or living. All gifts were treated alike, except a conjugal bequest, in which case, one half was exempted from the tax. The principle of individualism also permeated the field of income tax, in regard to the question of exemption for dependents and aggregate family income. In the estate tax, even in Europe, family relationship was considered; in the new Japanese tax law it was practically disregarded, whereas the individual's property and income was strongly emphasized. This total abandonment of the traditional feudalistic family system was extremely difficult to adjust to all at once. It would be desirable to give these inherent customs or usages due weight, without impairing the spirit of the reform.

INTRODUCTION OF A POLICY FOR BUSINESS ACTIVITIES

A policy designed to induce business revival was also woven into the reform. The revaluation of assets was one of the aspects of the policy for business prosperity. Revaluation does not entail an increase in the intrinsic value of assets but constitutes a devaluation of the currency which measures the value of property. Nevertheless, its effect is to make assets seem greater, although not a yen has been added to their intrinsic value. This fact should not cause confusion. The relation between the true value of assets and the value of depreciated money can be compared with that of the sun and the earth: because the earth moves, it looks as though the sun moves. Revaluation of assets will correct a similar illusion and incidentally it will play a very important role in the revival of business, because the illusion has interfered with sound business activities.

New legislation was recommended by the Shoup Mission to correct this. The purpose in enacting a new assets-revaluation law was to revalue corporate and individual assets and to eliminate abnormal accounting of enterprises. Provision was made for appropriate depreciation, and, by establishing a special treatment of taxation, a fair tax burden was sought for transfers of assets, all of which contributed to a normal economic operation.

As an example of capital gains, if a piece of land bought at 10,000 yen is sold at 1 million yen, one is apt to imagine that there is a gain of

990,000 yen. The new law did not interpret the matter so simply. If, due to inflation, all commodity prices went up ninety times, this particular piece of land would have the value of 900,000 yen; and up to that amount no gain is involved. Above that amount the gain is only 100,000 yen, that is, the difference between 1 million yen and 900,000 yen. On the other hand, if commodity prices had advanced 110 times and the land was disposed of at 1 million yen, this would be a capital loss of 100,000 yen. Any real gain from capital transfer had, of course, to be added to the amount of income as a capital gain, but a loss from transfer would, according to the reform, be subtracted from the income as a capital loss. There is little precedent for such a bold consideration of price fluctuations in the assessment of income tax and corporation tax. The purpose was to bring about a close relation between taxation and economic conditions.

TABLE 20

NATIONAL TAX SYSTEM BEFORE AND AFTER THE SHOUP RECOMMENDATIONS

1948	*1951*
Revenue Taxes	
Income	Income
Corporation	Corporation
Special corporation	Accession
Estate	Net worth
Capital levy	Revaluation
War indemnity	
Non-war sufferers'	
Circulation Taxes	
Securities transfer	Bourse
Transaction	Commodity
Bourse	Tonnage dues
Commodity	Travel
Tonnage	Registration
Travel	Stamp
Horse racing	
Registration	
Stamp	
Consumption Taxes	
Liquor	Liquor
Soft drinks	Monopoly profit
Monopoly profit	Sugar excise
Sugar excise	Playing sets
Textile excise	Gasoline
Playing sets	Customs duties
Customs duties	

CONCLUSION

So far I have pointed out several characteristics of the Shoup recommendations. I believe that Dr. Shoup's proposed tax reform is a splendid achievement which we can be proud to hand down to posterity. When I met Dr. Shoup a second time I told him that the Japanese people were heartily awaiting his visit. He replied that history shows that no one who attempted a tax reform was ever appreciated by his own generation. He meant, I believe, that although he might be criticized by the people of today, he trusted that his work might be of great significance to future generations of Japanese people.

The Shoup tax system is not the American tax system forced upon

TABLE 21

PREFECTURAL TAX SYSTEM BEFORE AND AFTER THE SHOUP RECOMMENDATIONS

1948	*1951*
Ordinary Taxes	
Prefectural inhabitant	Value-added (enterprise and special net income)
Land	Admission
House	Amusement, eating and drinking
Enterprise	Automobile
Special net income	Mine-lot
Mine product	Fishing right
Admission	Hunting
Liquor consumption	Extra-legal ordinary
Electricity and gas	
Mine	
Vessel	
Automobile	
Railway	
Telephone subscription right	
Electric pole	
Real property acquisition	
Timber trade	
Fishing right	
Hunting	
Amusement, eating and drinking	
Mineral bath	
Extra-legal ordinary	
Special Purpose Taxes	
City planning	Tax on irrigation, land reclaim and others
Tax on irrigation, land reclaim and others	

TABLE 22

MUNICIPAL TAX SYSTEM BEFORE AND AFTER THE SHOUP RECOMMENDATIONS

ORDINARY TAXES

(*Surtax on Prefectural Taxes*)

1948	*1951*
Land	Inhabitant's
House	
Enterprise	Municipal property
Special net income	
Mine product	Bicycle
Admission	
Liquor consumption	Cart
Electricity and gas	
Mine-lot	Electricity and gas
Vessel	
Automobile	Mine product
Railway	
Telephone subscription right	Timber trade
Electric pole	
Acquisition of real property	Advertisement
Timber trade	
Fishing right	Mineral bath
Hunting	
Amusement, eating and drinking	Service-girl
Mineral bath	Extra-legal ordinary
Prefectural extra-legal ordinary	
(*Independent Taxes*)	
Municipal inhabitant's	
Boat	
Bicycle	
Cart	
Safe	
Butchery	
Advertisement	
Service-girl	
Employee	
Extra-legal ordinary	
SPECIAL PURPOSE TAXES	
City planning	Tax on irrigation, land reclaim and others
Tax on irrigation, land reclaim and others	Common facilities
Common facilities	

Japan. It is an ideal system based on Dr. Shoup's theory, which was made public over ten years ago, and on that of Dr. Vickrey, which was published more than a year ago.

A creditable tax system such as has rarely been seen in the history of taxation—an ideal tax system that has never been tried either in Europe or in America—is now being put into practice in Japan. It must be remembered that it will have to be erected in a country having a long tradition and still in a wartorn condition. However desirable a system it may be, it cannot be successfully practiced unless due consideration is given to the prevailing economic and social conditions of Japan. Unfortunately, Japan is still troubled by abnormal postwar conditions, economic as well as social, although there has been gradual improvement. The new plan requires careful handling under the circumstances. Hasty enforcement must particularly be avoided. It would be advisable to set up the proper order of application so that the people gradually become familiar with the spirit of the reform; otherwise reactionary factions may spoil it. After all, a big undertaking like this cannot be accomplished in a day. Of course, no matter what happens we must not drift away from the ideal, but I believe that the best result can be obtained by approaching the goal step by step, giving full weight to the present social and economic life of the country.

Considered in relation to the systems of other countries, particularly in relation to the inducement of foreign capital, Japan must ask how the systems of other countries would affect her own? Would not her too-drastic tax system encourage a flight of capital instead of inducing foreign investment in Japan? What effect will it have on international tax relations?

In old Japan, the laws were strongly enforced, whereas in new Japan, this is not likely to happen for some time to come. An ideal tax system will be set up in a country where legal authority is weak. How can an international adjustment be made to the less drastic tax systems of other countries?

There is no doubt in my mind as to the high ideal of the Shoup tax system; it is the most advanced system in the world. My only concern is how to foster the ideal and to make it work harmoniously in this country where a number of abnormalties still exist and where a new international relationship is still to be faced.

VI. *Recent Alterations in National and Local Tax Laws and Opinions about the Future Tax System*

AT the round table conference of the Annual Convention of the Japan Tax Association held in 1951, eleven experts representing the academic, business, and official fields were gathered. Opinions were freely expressed and several subjects were discussed to full extent.

REPORT OF ROUND TABLE CONFERENCE (CHAIRMAN: DR. SABURO SHIOMI)

A round table conference to re-examine the present taxation structure was held on September 10, which lasted a good three hours from 1:20 P.M. to 4:20 P.M. The ten members who were present are listed in the order of speeches made: Mr. Hanya Ito, Professor at Tokyo Commercial University; Mr. Takao Takeda, Professor at Tokyo University; Mr. Saichiro Kaneko, Executive Director of the Jujo Paper Mill; Mr. Seiichiro Arai, Administrative Inspection Committee; Mr. Yoshimi Yamada, Director of the Hypothec Bank of Japan; Mr. Yasusaburo Hara, President of the Nippon Explosives Manufacturing Co.; Mr. Kanichi Moroi, Chairman of the Board of the Chichibu Cement Co.; Mr. Tamotsu Ogita, Director of the Local Finance Committee; Mr. Keiichiro Hirata, Director of the Taxation Bureau of the Finance Ministry; Mr. Hideo Matsukuma, President of the Central Liquors Co.

The present taxation structure in Japan was established on the recommendation of Dr. Shoup's Mission. For a long period, including the war interval, Japanese finance had been extremely centralized, national taxes occupying a predominant position in revenues, with local taxes subordinate to them. The position was so drastically changed by the Shoup recommendations that, in principle, government functions should be the responsibility of municipalities, and only those beyond municipal capacity should be handled by prefectures; others that neither municipalities nor prefectures can manage should be in the hands of the national government. In short, the principle of local independence in finance was established.

Many indirect taxes, both national and local, were abolished, among them the textile excise tax and the transaction tax in the field of national taxes, and taxes on acquisition of real property, automobiles, and bicycles in the field of local taxes. At the same time, special emphasis was placed on taxation of income through the income tax, corporation tax, and inhabitant tax, founding a tax system of which the backbone was direct taxes. While the top rate of the income tax was reduced, two new taxes were created: a national tax on property, called the net-worth tax; and a municipal tax (called the fixed-assets tax or municipal property tax) which covered an extensive variety of property. To coordinate the corporation and income taxes, a revolutionary system never practiced elsewhere was adopted. The value-added tax, one of the prefectural taxes, was also an innovation.

In the year following the institution of this new tax system, there had been a growing sentiment for its re-examination, the chief motive being the economic stringency in Japan. In the present feeble economic condition of a country scarcely recovered from war damages, the tax burden was altogether too heavy to permit stabilized life and the accumulation of capital. Another reason was that the highly idealistic Anglo-American system is not only unfamiliar but confusing to the Japanese nationals who have been accustomed to the Continental tax system for many years. Several questions were being raised: Should the taxation structure be centralized or decentralized? Should the government collect the major part of revenues from direct taxes or indirect taxes? Is the new value-added tax an improvement?

In view of the fact that Dr. Shoup, an adviser of our Association, had recommended the present system on a permanent basis as one of the best tax systems in the world, we felt we ought to foster it as it was, but the facts are that not only have the social and economic circumstances of the country changed since Dr. Shoup's return to the United States, but experience suggests that some of the provisions are not suitable to Japanese life. The National and Local Tax Committees of the Association, therefore, took up the matter and tried to reconcile the dissatisfaction voiced at the round table conference. I shall summarize under four headings: general discussion, national taxation structure, local taxation structure, and items common to both.

Fundamental problems in Japan's tax structure. The opinion was advanced that the national and local structures should be set up after the problem of distributing governmental functions between the national and local governments has been settled. In the meanwhile, the directly opposite opinion was also heard that since the distribution of functions was bound to change from time to time, the tax structure should first be set up and functions distributed accordingly. "How to deal with the present tax structure" was the next topic. The majority were in favor of maintaining the system in principle, with necessary modifications to meet the inconveniences and unrealities that occurred in practice. Some also held that a full-scale tax revision at this time should be avoided because of the great number of reforms that had been effected in recent years and that we should now be satisfied with partial amendments in the tax structure to suit current circumstances. One member was strongly in favor of scrapping the whole system and returning to the prewar system as the basic structure.

Problems of national taxation. In discussing the problem of relative weight on direct and indirect taxes, a majority seemed to believe that the present system depended too heavily on direct taxes. It would be the ideal form of taxation to raise the bulk of revenues from direct taxes, but social, economic, and other conditions in Japan lack the prerequisites for such a system. It is admitted that our economic mechanism is in a stage of fairly advanced capitalism, but at the same time the capital accumulation is at its lowest point and urgently needs to be augmented. Under these circumstances, a tax system that relies so greatly on the income tax involves many contradictions. It was suggested that some exceptions should be made in levying this tax, that the progressive rate should be lowered, and that the relative weight on indirect or excise taxes should be increased. In this connection it was pointed out that the ratio of direct taxes to the total tax revenue was 85 percent in the United States, 56 percent in England, 22 percent in Italy, and 54 percent in Japan. Another member, supporting the present system, expressed the view that indirect taxes should be confined only to luxury items, and that commodity taxes should be avoided, lest they have an ill effect on commodity prices.

As to the corporation tax, there was strong opposition to any increase, in view of the need for greater capital accumulation. Since the tax burden on corporations and individuals is well balanced under the present system and the corporation tax is netting a larger revenue than anticipated, any proposal to raise the corporation tax must be avoided. The present corporation tax of nearly 60 percent (the combined corporation tax, enterprise tax, and inhabitant tax is 59.25 percent) is already too high and should rather be lowered to encourage the accumulation of capital.

Next came the net-worth tax. The general opinion was that it was not worthwhile to keep it because it yielded too little revenue and was administratively too troublesome to enforce. The deficit of revenues could easily be met by raising the top rate of the income tax.

In discussing the accession tax, it was insisted that this should be so lowered as to suit actual conditions in Japan. Special attention was drawn to the fact that in the United States the top rates of the income tax and accession tax were 91 percent and 80 percent, respectively, whereas those in Japan were the other way round, 55 percent and 90 percent, respectively.

Problems of local taxation. This was an area of heated controversy. While the present allocation of revenue sources between national and local governments was supported by some members, many others disagreed. Generally speaking, national taxes had had fair sailing so far, but local taxes still presented many problems to be adjusted. Had the local independent taxes sufficient backing under the present financial status of local governments? Could local governments be financially independent with their own revenue sources? It is actual current practice that any data collected by the national tax offices for the purpose of assessing tax are used unchanged, by the local tax offices, because the tax administration of local governments is too inefficient to amend them. There was no question but what local bodies must be strengthened, but it was pointed out that this must be done step by step in a country like Japan. In the matter of prefectural taxes, it was argued that, since revenue sources of prefectures are concentrated in cities, other sources should be discovered to make all inhabitants in the prefectures share the tax burden.

As to the valuc-added tax, some were in favor of it in theory, while others were against it as impractical, although they were dissatisfied with the present enterprise tax as it is. A suggestion was made to utilize external indicia in assessing the tax, although there was no consensus as to whether the standard should be the amount of sales, the amount of wages, or the amount of value added.

The fixed asset tax or municipal property tax was also brought on the agenda. A member insisted that it should be treated as a prefectural tax, allowing municipalities to levy a surtax on it. Another proposal was to bring the fixed asset tax back to the old land tax and the house tax, and not to levy it on depreciable assets.

In regard to Local Finance Equalization Grants allowed to local bodies from the national treasury, it was contended that local finance should, in principle, rely on its own sources of revenue, with disparities adjusted by a grant from the central government. Educational expense should also, as a rule, be borne locally and only the deficit should be made up out of national funds.

Problems common to national and local taxation. These comprised the heavy tax burden, curtailment of expenses, and capital accumulation. One member opined that under the present system, the progressive rates and basic exemptions, particularly those of the income tax and the accession tax, have been distorted by inflation and need a fundamental re-examination. The present tax burden, both direct and indirect, has already reached the breaking point. An example in the field of indirect taxation is the fact that the recent price cut in tobacco actually increased the monopoly revenue. The case of direct taxes is not so clearly demonstrated, but the many tax evasions can be taken as endorsement of the view. At any rate, it is an urgent necessity to reduce the income tax, particularly on earned income. The question naturally arises as to how to make up the resultant deficit and how to curtail expenditures. Someone suggested that the newly adopted education system (six grades plus three grades, or the "6-3 system") should be done away with. The question of tax cut cannot be solved unless it is preceded by expenditure cut. Apart from several items which are bound to increase in the future (in connection with international relations and defense), there are several areas in which expenditures could be cut as in government investment, education, social welfare, and public works. How should these expenditures be adjusted or curtailed? It was concluded that unless these questions are first settled, the tax problem would remain unsolved.

All present agreed that accumulation of capital was the matter of most urgent necessity. In general, Japanese industry is hard put to maintain present equipment, to say nothing of expanding it. In order to feed millions of surplus overpopulation in a very small territory, international trade is the only hope and, for that, capital is desperately needed. The national and local tax systems are making it difficult to attain this objective. What is needed, therefore, is to incorporate an economic policy into a taxation policy on full scale.

Ratio between direct and indirect taxes. After all the reports were made, the remaining time was used for free debate among the members. A summary of the discussion follows.

The ratio between direct and indirect taxes was the fundamental issue in the re-examination of the taxation structure. It has been commented that, ideal as the Shoup tax system is, Japanese social and economic conditions do not provide a solid foundation for its successful practice. Most business leaders, as well as the academic representatives present, concurred in this view, saying that the system was far too advanced for the Japanese people, whose conservative mind is set on the old-fashioned concept that an old tax is a good tax, a new tax is bad tax, and that all light taxes are good, all heavy taxes are bad. Since this was the opinion expressed by leading men in various fields, it should not be altogether ignored but should be considered carefully. It was suggested that indirect taxes be increased by reducing direct taxes, but the question of which indirect taxes should be raised went unanswered. Many related problems, such as the sales tax, capital accumulation, rates of income tax and the top rate, net-worth tax, and the Japanese tax burden as compared with that of other countries were also extensively and technically discussed.

Since the round table discussion, economic conditions have changed, a part of the tax system has been revised, some of the author's suggestions have been accepted and others left untouched. In the light of the admitted superiority of the system itself and the permanency it aims at, its fundamentals must at any cost be retained, but some appropriate revisions in a transition period are necessary. The revisions made after 1950 were mostly of that nature.

RECENT ALTERATIONS

In 1951 certain revisions were performed, some of them regarding the individual income tax, at the recommendation of the second Shoup Mission (1950). In regard to the income tax, the amount of deduction was increased, the rates were reduced, and a special reduction was made for individuals.

As to the corporation tax, the tax on reserves other than family corporations was repealed, amortization was allowed for certain machineries and equipments, a second revaluation of assets was carried out, and the rates of indirect taxes were adjusted.

In 1952 the revision chiefly concerned the income tax and the corporation tax: the basic reduction and dependency exemption were increased; the tax on retirement income was reduced; the withholding system on dividends was restored; the rate of corporation tax was raised to 42 percent; and the depreciation method was rationalized. For local taxes, the basic exemption of 38,000 yen in the enterprise tax was established; the rates of the admissions tax and the amusement, eating and drinking tax were reduced, as was the corporation rate of inhabitant tax; and the fishing right tax, the advertisement tax, and service girl tax were repealed.

In 1953 the basic exemption and dependency exemption were increased for the income tax. The tax rate for higher wage earners was raised, whereas the taxation of capital gains of securities was repealed. In regard to the corporation tax, a tax on liquidation income was set up, the net-worth tax was repealed, the accession tax was divided into an inheritance tax and gift tax, and the third revaluation of assets was made. A fundamental revision of the liquor tax law was made, and the securities transaction tax newly introduced. In local taxes there were increases in the basic exemption of the enterprise tax, and in the rate of the inhabitant tax, the automobile tax, the mine-lot tax, and the mineral bath tax.

In 1954, the tax system was again reformed broadly in national as well as local taxes, at the recommendation of the Tax System Research Council and the Local Autonomy System Research Council established by the Cabinet. The changes affected the income tax in several ways; it increased the rates of the basic exemption, dependency credit, and the exemption for retirement income; rationalized the taxation on forestry income; reduced the withholding tax rate on dividend income; and introduced the prepayment system in order to simplify the self-assessment system. Changes in the corporation tax introduced a special measure to lighten the tax if the corporations' capital increase was made under certain conditions, repealed the tax system for the accumulated reserves of family corporations (replacing it with a once-and-for-all levy of 10 percent instead of a charge for each fiscal year), rationalized the price fluctuation reserve system, and restricted the entertainment expenses of corporations. For the accession tax, the amount of reduction for the proceeds of life insurance and retirement income was increased, and the tax rates were decreased. With respect to indirect taxes, the tax rates of the liquor tax, the sugar excise, the commodity tax, the gasoline tax, and the playing-set tax were raised to some extent, and the admissions tax was transferred to national tax.

To avoid double taxation and to forestall tax evasion, a tax agreement was concluded between the United States and Japan on the income, the corporation, and the accession taxes. The agreement has been in operation since January 1, 1954.

The 1954 revision also affected several aspects of local taxes; 1) the inhabitant's tax, which had been limited to municipalities, was extended to prefectures; 2) the enterprise tax replaced the value-added tax; 3) the real estate acquisition tax was established as a prefectural tax; 4) a certain portion of the retail price of tobacco was given to prefectures and municipalities under the name of the tobacco-consumption tax; 5) the amusement facilities-using tax was created as a prefectural tax.

It is noteworthy that the local distributive tax system was adopted in lieu of the local finance equalization grants, and that a new system of the refund tax was established. The amount of local distributive taxes was set as a fixed portion of the income, corporation, and liquor taxes, whereas the amount of the local finance equalization grants varied every fiscal year. The refund tax is a mixture of local independent and local distributive taxes; 90 percent of the admissions tax collected by the national tax administration agency is returned to the prefectures in proportion to population.

In 1955, the latest reform was made, chiefly to reduce the rate of direct taxes. It had become evident that the burden of direct taxes was interferring with badly needed capital accumulation and also stabilized living. The new reform covered a number of items, chiefly in fields already subjected to changes.

For the income tax, the amount of basic exemption was raised, as were the credit for earned income and the maximum deduction for insurance premium. The rate for small incomes and the withholding rate for dividends was lowered. The tax on income from interest was repealed. Special benefits for "blue return" (tax return made in accordance with the formula prescribed by the tax office) were enlarged. An innovation was made to allow a lump-sum deduction for medical expenses, social insurance premiums, and other casual losses, instead of a separate claim for each of these.

Concerning the corporation tax, the rate was lowered to 35 percent on incomes less than 500,000 yen and to 40 percent on the portion above that amount. The rate for liquidation income was lowered. The depreciation rate for new houses built for rental purposes was raised. To promote the housing program, the registration tax was either reduced or eliminated for houses built under certain conditions. The transportation tax was reduced for travel by plane. The excise tax was adjusted as to the rates of the sugar excise on various grades. Lastly, the local road tax on gasoline was created to raise a fund for local road-building and repairing.

The taxation system in Japan set up at the recommendation of Dr. Shoup's Mission in 1950 was modified every year from 1951 on, to suit actual conditions, but the fundamental idea of the system has been upheld in the light of its superiority and permanence.

During the past fifteen years, the number of national taxes enforced at one time or an other has reached as many as thirty-eight. Some of these have been in force during the entire fifteen years; some lived only a year.

Number of Taxes	*Number of Years Enforced*
11	15
5	10
5	8
4	7
3	9
3	5
2	3
2	1
1	12
1	4
1	2
38	

TAXATION OF ALIENS AND FOREIGN CORPORATIONS

Generally speaking, an alien must pay various Japanese taxes the same as Japanese nationals do. An alien who has domicile or who has resided for one year or more in Japan is subject to taxes on his income wherever it accrues. An alien who has neither domicile nor residence in Japan or who has resided for less than one year in Japan, on the other hand, is taxed only on that part of his income which is derived from sources within Japan. The special tax concession measures, in-

TABLE 23

LIST OF NATIONAL TAXES AND TIME WHEN ENFORCED DURING THE PAST FIFTEEN YEARS

(x = enforced)

National Taxes	*1940*	*1941*	*1942*	*1943*	*1944*	*1945*	*1946*	*1947*	*1948*	*1949*	*1950*	*1951*	*1952*	*1953*	*1954*
Income	x	x	x	x	x	x	x	x	x	x	x	x	x	x	x
Corporation	x	x	x	x	x	x	x	x	x	x	x	x	x	x	x
Estate (accession)	x	x	x	x	x	x	x	x	x	x	x	x	x	x	x
Travel	x	x	x	x	x	x	x	x	x	x	x	x	x	x	x
Registration	x	x	x	x	x	x	x	x	x	x	x	x	x	x	x
Liquor	x	x	x	x	x	x	x	x	x	x	x	x	x	x	x
Sugar excise	x	x	x	x	x	x	x	x	x	x	x	x	x	x	x
Bourse	x	x	x	x	x	x	x	x	x	x	x	x	x	x	x
Stamp	x	x	x	x	x	x	x	x	x	x	x	x	x	x	x
Playing sets	x	x	x	x	x	x	x	x	x	x	x	x	x	x	x
Commodity	x	x	x	x	x	x	x	x	x	x	x	x	x	x	x
Securities transfer to 1949 (Securities transaction, 1953–54)	x	x	x	x	x	x	x	x	x	x				x	x
Transaction	x	x	x	x	x	x	x	x	x	x					
Soft drinks	x	x	x	x	x	x	x	x	x	x					
Textile excise	x	x	x	x	x	x	x	x	x	x					
Special corporation	x	x	x	x	x	x	x	x	x						
Admission	x	x	x	x	x	x	x	x	x						x
Hunting license	x	x	x	x	x	x	x	x	x						
Horse racing	x	x	x	x	x	x	x	x	x						
Land	x	x	x	x	x	x	x	x							

House	x	x	x	x	x	x	x	x							
Business (business profit)	x	x	x	x	x	x	x	x							
Mine-lot	x	x	x	x	x	x	x	x							
Amusement, eating and drinking	x	x	x	x	x	x	x	x							
Special tax on dividends and interest	x	x	x	x	x	x	x								
Special tax on bonds in foreign currency	x	x	x	x	x	x	x								
Extraordinary profit	x	x	x	x	x	x	x								
Building	x	x	x	x	x	x	x								
Gasoline	x	x	x	x						x	x	x	x	x	x
Convertible note issue	x	x	x												
Electricity and gas			x	x	x	x	x								
Advertisement			x	x	x	x	x								
Special act				x	x	x	x								
Capital levy							x								
War indemnity							x								
Non-war sufferers								x	x						
Net-worth											x	x	x		
Revaluation											x	x	x	x	x
Number	30	30	32	32	31	31	33	25	20	16	14	14	14	14	15

cluding so called "one-half deduction" hitherto provided for, expired on December 31, 1955. As a temporary measure of the transitional period, however, a new tax relief provision is made for special earned income, effective until the 1960 calendar year, the details of which are explained below. The particulars of the new tax regulations for aliens and foreign corporations are as follows:

Alien Individuals

INCOME TAX

1. An alien who has domicile or has resided in Japan more than one year. Such an alien is taxed the same as Japanese nationals on all his income (including income from sources outside Japan) received during the calendar year. In computing the tax amount, firstly, each income (dividend income, real estate income, business income, earned income, retirement income, forestry income, capital gains, temporary income, and other miscellaneous income) is determined on the full calendar year basis, January to December; secondly, the total amount of taxable income is obtained from the total amount of the above enumerated incomes (excluding retirement income and forestry income), after such deductions and exemptions as listed below:

(*a*) Basic exemption 90,000 yen.

(*b*) Exemption for dependents, 50,000 yen for the first dependent, 25,000 yen each for the second and third dependent, 15,000 yen per person for the rest.

(*c*) Deduction for life insurance premium, 22,500 yen maximum.

(*d*) Deduction for miscellaneous losses caused by calamities such as storm, fire, or others.

(*e*) Deduction for medical expenses (for the amount in excess of 5 percent of the total income: maximum, 150,000 yen).

(*f*) Deduction for social security (insurance premium).

And finally, the tax amount is computed by applying the ordinary tax rates to such net taxable amount as obtained above. The tax amount on retirement income is separately computed by applying the same tax rates on one half of the income, after deducting 200,000 yen plus 20,000 yen per year if his service exceeds ten years, provided, however that the total amount of such deductions should not exceed 500,000 yen. Interest income is exempt until 1957. In payment of taxes, the self-assessment or provisional payment system is generally applied, except that the taxes on earned income, retirement income, dividend income and so on are withheld at the source at the time of payment.

2. The special alien wage earner who has resided more than one year but has no domicile in Japan. A special concession effective until the 1960 calendar year is allowed to the following groups of earned income paid to an alien who has resided more than one year but who has no domicile in Japan:

(*a*) Earned income paid to employees of a corporation which is engaged in business designated by the Minister of Finance as contributing to the development of Japanese economy.

(*b*) Earned income paid to employees of a corporation which is engaged in scientific, educational, or other nonprofit activities, designated by the Minister of Finance as serving the promotion of culture.

(*c*) Earned income paid to professors and teachers of a university, college, or high school.

(*d*) Earned income paid to ministers or missionaries of a religious organization.

On such incomes as mentioned above, the income tax is not imposed if the payment of the income is made outside of Japan. Any remittance to Japan out of such income, however, is construed as an income in Japan and is subject to the income tax. If the normal expenses for living exceed the total income in Japan, such an excess is liable to be taxed to the extent of earned income outside of Japan less remittance to Japan therefrom. The concession allowed for taxable income amount is as follows:

1957, to be taxed on 60% of total income
1958, to be taxed on 70% of total income
1959, to be taxed on 80% of total income
1960, to be taxed on 90% of total income

The ordinary income tax rates are to be applied. The method of tax payment is similar to that of "1."

3. An alien who has neither domicile nor residence for one year or more in Japan. Such an alien who comes under any one of the following categories is liable to the Japanese income tax on his income derived from sources in Japan:

(*a*) An alien who receives income from assets or enterprises located in Japan.

(*b*) An alien who receives interest on Japanese government bonds, local bonds, or corporate debentures (will be exempted until 1957).

(*c*) An alien who receives interest on bank deposits or profit from joint-operation trusts (interest will be exempted until 1957).

(*d*) An alien who receives dividends from Japanese corporations or distribution of gains from securities investment trust operated by Japanese corporation.

(*e*) An alien who earns income or receives remuneration for his service rendered in Japan.

(*f*) An alien who receives royalties for industrial ownership rights, technical rights, or copyrights (including projecting right on movie films) from a person engaged in enterprise in Japan.

(*g*) An alien who receives interest on loans to a person engaged in enterprise in Japan.

(*h*) An alien who receives income from real properties or leasehold of quarrying right in Japan.

The income of (*a*) is taxed by the method of self-assessment or provisional payment while other incomes are taxed at sources at the rate of 20 percent. The dividend income is taxed at the rate of 10 percent until 1957. For interest income, dividend of shares or profit distributed on investment which are legally acquired in foreign currency, the rate is reduced to 10 percent for the time being.

ACCESSION TAX

The accession tax, under the present system, is divided into the accession tax and the gift tax. Assessment of the accession tax is the value of property acquired by succession minus 500,000 yen, and the rates progress from the low of 10 percent on the amount less than 200,000 yen to the high of 70 percent on the amount over 100 million yen. No accession tax is imposed on properties used for public welfare.

One half amount of the value of property acquired by succession from a spouse is excluded from assessment. If a successor has domicile in Japan and is a minor, the amount deductible from assessment is computed by multiplying 20,000 yen by the number of years required for him to reach eighteen.

If a person who acquired properties by succession had, within two years of succession, received other properties as a gift from the person whom he succeeded, the value of the gift-properties shall be included in his income.

A person who is heir to properties for which the accession tax has already been paid once within the last ten years may deduct an amount computed by multiplying one tenth of the paid tax by the difference between ten years and the number of years elapsed since the first succession. Credit may be allowed for the estate tax (similar to the Japanese accession tax) paid to a foreign government on property inherited in Japan.

The assessment of the gift tax is the amount of value of properties acquired by gift or bequest minus 100,000 yen, and the rates progress from the low of 10 percent on less than 200,000 yen to the high 70 percent on more than 30 million yen. No gift tax is imposed on properties given by a juridical person or on properties to be used for public welfare.

EXCISE

All imported commodities are subject to Japanese excises (liquor commodities, sugar, playing sets, gasoline). No excise is imposed on commodities procured for official purposes by the United States armed forces or by authorized procurement agencies, for members of the United States armed forces and civilians attached to the forces, or on those imported as personal effects by ordinary aliens (except liquors) or for official purposes by diplomatic missions or for self-use by members of diplomatic missions.

Commodities released by the United States armed forces are subject to the commodity tax. If an alien transfers a motor vehicle to another alien, he must pay the commodity tax unless it can be proved that the tax has already been paid on the vehicle in question.

All domestic commodities are subject to excise, except those purchased by the armed forces or authorized procurement agencies.

An alien who desires to manufacture or sell liquor must obtain a permit from the chief of the tax office. A person who desires to manufacture or sell such commodities as sugar, playing-sets and others that are subject to the commodity tax must file an application to the chief of the tax office.

PREFECTURAL INHABITANT'S TAX

The prefectural inhabitant's tax is imposed on an alien inhabitant of a metropolis or a prefecture. It is levied on a per capita basis and income basis. The standard rate is 100 yen per capita and 5 percent of the preceding year's income.

MUNICIPAL INHABITANT'S TAX

The municipal inhabitant's tax, in principle, is levied on inhabitants in cities, towns, and villages, on a per capita and income basis. For this, standard per capita rates are: 600 yen in cities with population over 500,000; 400 yen in cities with population over 50,000 but less than 500,000; 200 yen in all other cities, towns, and villages. As to the income basis, the taxing authority may choose one of these alternatives: 15 percent of the amount of income tax for the preceding year; 7.5 percent of the total taxable income for the preceding year; 15 percent of the total taxable income less the amount of income tax for the preceding year.

The municipal property tax is imposed on land, houses, and other depreciable assets on the basis of the fair market value of properties. The rate was 1.4 percent for 1955 and thereafter.

The real property acquisition tax is imposed on acquisition of real properties at the rate of 3 percent of the fair market value.

The enterprise tax on the owner or operator of an enterprise is levied by prefectures where the place of business is located. The standard rates are: Class I, 6 percent of the taxable amount (income minus 120,000 yen) not exceeding 500,000 yen, 8 percent of taxable amount over 500,000 yen; Classes II and III, 6 percent of the taxable income of the preceding year, 4 percent for certain activities.

Alien Corporations

CORPORATION TAX

A corporation having its head office or principal places of business in Japan is liable to the corporation tax. If the head office or principal places of business is not in Japan (foreign corporation), it is subject to the corporation tax only on income accrued from assets or business in Japan. A foreign corporation is not subject to tax on its liquidation income. The corporation tax is charged at the rate of 35 percent on the amount of income less than 1 million yen and 40 percent on the part of income exceeding 1 million yen for each accounting period and is calculated by deducting gross expenses from gross income.

INCOME TAX

If a corporation receives income from any of the items enumerated for individuals of group C or income from real property or leasehold of quarrying right in Japan, it is subject to income tax at the rate of 20 percent, collectible at the source at the time of payment.

EXCISES

The regulations for excises payable by corporations are the same as those for individuals.

PREFECTURAL INHABITANT'S TAX

The prefectural inhabitant's tax is imposed on a corporation by the metropolis or prefecture in which the head office or place of business is located. The tax is levied on a per capita basis and corporation tax basis. The standard rates are 600 yen per capita basis and 5.4 percent of the amount of corporation tax (maximum 6.5 percent).

MUNICIPAL INHABITANT'S TAX

This tax is levied on corporations having an office or business place in Japan on a per capita basis and the corporation tax basis. For the per capita basis the standard rates are based on population. For each office or business place in cities of over 500,000, they are 2,400 yen; in cities of over 50,000 but less than 500,000, they are 1,800 yen; in others they are 1,200 yen. For the corporation tax basis, the rates are 8.1 percent of the amount of corporation tax.

MUNICIPAL PROPERTY TAX AND PROPERTY ACQUISITION TAX

The regulations for the payment of municipal property and property acquisition taxes are the same as those for individuals.

ENTERPRISE TAX

A corporation is taxed under the enterprise tax on the receipts or net income of each accounting period and also on its liquidation income. The standard rates are according to type of enterprise. For electricity or gas suppliers, casualty and life insurance businesses, they are 1.5 percent of receipts. For other businesses such as special corporations (e. g. an agricultural cooperative association), they are 8 percent of the net income and liquidation income, and for ordinary corporations, they are 8 percent for income less than 500,000 yen, 10 percent for income less than 1 million yen, and 12 percent for income over 1 million yen.

PART THREE

The Establishment and Development of the Income Tax and the Corporation Tax

VII. *The Japanese Tax System Studied through the Development of the Income Tax*

IN previous chapters, the author has described the economic development in Japan that formed the background of Japanese finance, and the development of the national and local tax systems. In this chapter we will study the characteristics of Japanese finance by concentrating on the development of the income tax, for it is the income tax that is usually found as the nucleus of the taxation system in advanced countries, and its development in Japan most convincingly explains the characteristics of Japanese finance.

The development of the tax may be conveniently divided into seven periods. In the first period, 1887 to 1899, the income tax was first created (1887); and the Sino-Japanese war was waged (1894 to 1895). In the second period, 1899 to 1913, a new law which laid the foundation of the income tax system was enacted (1899); and the Emergency Special Taxation Law was promulgated during the Russo-Japanese war (1904 to 1905). In the third period, 1913 to 1920, the Emergency Special Taxation Law was withdrawn (1913) and modern principles were gradually incorporated; this period also covered World War I. In the fourth period, 1920 to 1940, modernization of the tax was carried out for the first time (1920) and the resultant stabilization lasted until 1940; at the close of the period, however, certain revisions were made as a result of the outbreak of the Manchurian and China struggles. The fifth period, 1940 to 1945, witnessed the adoption of a new law in 1940; during most of these years Japan was embroiled in World War II. In the sixth period, 1946 to 1950, emergency measures were enforced one after the other to deal with the aftermath of the war. The seventh period, from 1950 on, covers the years following the revolutionary reform of the entire taxation system as recommended by Dr. Shoup in 1949 and 1950.

THE FIRST PERIOD, 1887-1899
CREATION OF THE INCOME TAX

Influence of Rudolff's draft of the revenue tax. Japan's income tax was first established by the law promulgated in March, 1887. Its immediate purpose was to alleviate the tax on certain products in Hokkaido, although at the time, Japan had been undergoing rapid national development and was facing the necessity of expanding her naval forces at the cost of ever-increasing government expenditures. Hitherto, Japan had depended on her traditional taxes—land and liquor. The adoption of the income tax, therefore, was the first step toward the creation of a modern system. As a student of comparative finance, the author was naturally interested in knowing how we came to be influenced by the Western system.

The first income tax law was presented to the Cabinet Council in January, 1887; it was promulgated on March 23 by Imperial Ordinance No. 5, after being somewhat modified by the Council of State.

Referring to Count Masayoshi Matsukata's "Principles of the Income Tax Law," Professor Isamu Abe asserts that the income tax law draft prepared by the Count in December, 1884, was the basis of the first income tax law in Japan. But this writer holds a different view. On the evidence of an older record, obtained through the courtesy of Mr. Takatate of the Library of the Department of Finance, he is inclined to believe that a draft of the revenue tax law presented in a letter dated November 29, 1874, to Hirobumi Ito, a member of the Council of State, and written by a German financial adviser named Rudolff, was the real basis of our income tax law. In the letter, Rudolff asked Ito to entrust him with the work of preparing a draft for the promulgation of the revenue tax law in 1875. Rudolff stated that, following instructions from Hirobumi Ito, he had exempted the income from land on which the land tax was imposed and also the income from liquor production, but that his list included all miscellaneous incomes. Ten years later, Miyoji Ito, secretary, after having consulted with Rudolff and another German financial expert named Roesler, presented a letter to Hirobumi Ito expressing his views on the current problems of this particular form of taxation. At the same time, Miyoji Ito presented to Hirobumi Ito a number of translations of tax law drafts and German tax laws. It is a fact that the revenue tax law was made with the advice of these two German experts and the substance of Rudolff's draft greatly resembled that of the German income tax law; and it is clear that this draft influenced, at least indirectly, the income tax law of 1887. This is the basis for the writer's contention that Japan adopted the ideas of the Western tax system in the establishment of her first income tax law.

Features of the law of 1887. Let us compare the provisions of 1887 with those of Rudolff's draft of the revenue tax. The two agree in general structure but differ in many minor points. Article 1 of the income tax law fixes the exemption limit at 300 yen as compared with 400 yen in Rudolff's draft. But this exemption point was raised to 400 yen in 1913. The revenue tax law draft was detailed in regard to the domicile of alien taxpayers and the locale of tax objects, but these were omitted in the income tax law, either because Japan's relations with foreign countries were very simple then or because she had to be careful about the sentiments of foreign powers. With these minor differences, the spirit of the revenue tax law draft, as expressed by Rudolff, was embodied in the new law of 1899.

The method of calculating incomes as provided in Article 2 of the first law was the same as that of the draft in respect to the principle of averaging three years' actual income. This was temporarily replaced by the principle of estimation in 1899 but was restored in 1926, when the estimate was restricted to the actual income of the preceding year.

Whereas the rates of the 1887 law were on a simple basis of progressive percentage (which lasted until 1913), those of the revenue draft were on a simple basis of progressive amount. The former is logically superior in applying percentages, but has the disadvantage of a smaller number of progressive brackets than the latter. The provision relating to the domestic circumstances of taxpayers as provided by the revenue draft was not incorporated in the first law; it was adopted in 1920.

While the revenue tax law draft and income tax law have their own respective features in regard to the time of payment (Article 5), obligation of declaration to the revenue office (Article 6), the county district income investigation commission (Article 7), the prefectural standing commission (Article 20), and reduction and revision (Article 23), there is no denying the close relationship between the two.

THE SECOND PERIOD, 1899-1912

FUNDAMENTAL REVISION OF THE FIRST INCOME TAX LAW

The enactment of the law of 1887 was a marked attempt to import foreign systems and institutions. In motivation it was regarded as a copy of a foreign system rather than the establishment of a workable

Japanese system. In order to make the law serve in its social environment it was necessary to curb its radical features and to supplement its insufficiencies. A remarkable improvement was that the taxation on corporate dividends and interest on bonds and debentures was brought back to the withholding-at-source system, that the stipulation for international taxation was provided for, and that the number of brackets for the Class III income (individual income) was increased. Just at that time the government needed a vast source of revenue to make up the huge fiscal deficits created in the period after the Sino-Japanese War. Accordingly, as soon as the 12th session of the Imperial Diet was opened in May, 1898, the government presented a bill for revising the income tax law. At a committee meeting on June 2, Mr. Reijiro Wakatsuki, the government delegate, explained the bill substantially as follows:

The Department of Finance has long felt the necessity of revising the income tax law, enacted in 1887 and now in force, because it has become out of date in its application to existing circumstances. Its defects are especially pronounced when the law is applied to foreigners. When the revised treaties take effect and if foreigners are taxed as provided for in these treaties, the income tax law must be revised by all means. Since corporations and individuals are altogether different, the tax should be imposed on both corporations and the individual citizens who receive dividends from them. Such a system of income taxation is being practiced in other countries. In spite of that fact, our proposed law taxes only corporations and does not tax individual taxpayers on their corporate dividends. The reason for this is more sentimental than logical: that taxation of both may give an impression of double taxation, although it is not so, as pointed out above. At any rate, we do not wish to go too far ahead in the present attempt at tax revision. We have, of course, no intention of unfairly levying the tax burden on corporations only.

The law of 1899. The bill was killed as the Diet dissolved in June, 1898. In November of the same year, another bill was presented to the 13th session as was adopted by the House of Representatives after some modification. The House of Peers was in favor of the bill in almost its original form and after remodifying it to that effect sent it back to the House of Representatives. It was there approved, and as modified by the House of Peers, the bill became law on February 10, 1899.

The bill presented to the 12th session of the Imperial Diet, retained something of the earlier law, inasmuch as it adopted the three-year average system in its Article 5. On the other hand, it included an advanced feature of dividing incomes into five classes, each with a progressive rate. Mr. Reijiro Wakatsuki, the government delegate, explained to the Diet about Articles 3 and 4 in substance as follows:

Theoretically speaking, all incomes should be taxed. But in practice, there are some exceptions that should be exempted from tax, such as specified in Article 3. Salaries paid to soldiers in wartime, temporary incomes, and incomes from individuals who pay the tax through their corporations are exempted under the provision. Referring to Article 4, some incomes are steady and can be secured without much labor, while others can only be obtained by hard toil. Again, other incomes are uncertain and irregular. Accordingly, incomes are classified into five groups and a different rate is imposed on each item in order to ensure a fair distribution of the tax burden. Corporate incomes (Class I) are entirely set apart from others because it is difficult to treat them like others, as they are determined at the time of corporation fiscal closing accounts. Classes II and III are incomes from either past labor or capital accumulated in the past. In other words, Class II is income from capital accumulated in the past and is the most secure of all; Class III, is a combination of income from capital earned in the past and labor of today; Class IV is income from ordinary labor; and all other incomes, such as pensions or annuities, come under Class V, the rate for which is higher than that of Class IV but lower than other classes as the nature of income calls for.

The bill failed to pass the Diet because of the dissolution of the House but the idea contained therein, namely, that corporate income (Class I) and interest on bonds and debentures (Class II) should be detached from other incomes (Class III), was reasserted in the bill presented to the 13th session of the Diet. This idea formed the basic structure of the income tax law for a long time. The House of Representatives modified the bill by merging Class II with Class III, but the House of Peers reverted to the original. The bill as adopted by the House of Peers was sent back to the House of Representatives and accepted. In explaining the restoration of the bill to its original form, Mr. Reijiro Wakatsuki stated that the House of Peers was right in accepting the principle that, so long as the tax is levied on corporate income at its source, it should also be levied on interest on bonds and debentures where it is paid.

This principle of detaching Class II income from Class III income had been in force in Japan for many years. Even after the withholding-at-source system was abandoned in part in 1920, when 60 percent dividend was added to individual income for the purpose of aggregate taxation, the Class II income maintained the principle established in 1899. The fundamental idea of the five-class income tax proposed at the 12th session of the Diet was adopted and put into actual practice, though the five classes were reduced to three when the bill was actually enacted in the following year.

The principle features of revision made by the 13th session of the Diet in 1899 were as follows:

1. The scope of taxpayers' obligation was defined as to domicile, residence, and location of taxable items.

2. The income tax was divided into three classes: Class I is corporate income (individuals are not taxed for dividends from corporations); Class II is interest on bonds and debentures and is taxed when and where it is paid out; Class III is individual income that does not belong in Class II.

3. The method of calculation was modified: Class I income is computed by deducting gross business expenses from gross income and is fixed by taking into consideration the valuation of corporate property and its depreciation; Class II is computed on the total amount received; Class III is computed by deducting from the total income all necessary expenditures and by taking annual estimates.

4. Tax rates were revised. The law adopted proportional rates for Classes I and II and progressive rates for Class III, for which a greater number of brackets was provided.

5. The right of investigation and assessment of income was transferred from the prefectures and counties to the Tax Affairs Supervision Bureau.

Emergency special taxes. In order to meet the expenditure of the Russo-Japanese War, the tax burden was greatly increased and the income tax law was revised twice. The first tax increase was made in 1904 by Law No. 3.

Upholding the idea that the income tax should be levied on persons of means, the amount of the tax on Classes I and III was increased by 70 percent of the original tax amount. Class II was exempted from this increase because the government wished to maintain the value of bonds at as high a level as possible. In 1905 the government formulated a plan to increase the rates by 80 percent. Since the first increase was 70 percent, the total became 150 percent. Class I incomes were divided into categories A and B. The former was defined as the incomes of joint-stock companies or joint-stock partnerships composed of more than twenty-one persons, shareholders and company officials combined. The rates of these incomes were increased by 80 percent. Incomes under B were defined as those of other corporations and were grouped into eight brackets, with rates increased by 10 percent to 640 percent progressively. Class III incomes were grouped into ten brackets, with rates increased by 30 percent to 200 percent progressively. The government expected to garner 5,862,240 yen by the second increase of the rates; but as the Diet modified the rates of B income under Class I, the amount was reduced to 5,286,462 yen. It is noteworthy that the second increase in the rates divided Class I into categories A and B. This division was necessary in order to forestall evasion of an individual tax through the formation of fictitious corporations.

Corporations having more than twenty-one shareholders and company officials combined were to pay proportional taxes as hitherto; while smaller corporations of a private nature were to pay progressive taxes according to respective individual incomes.

So far, the attitude of legislators toward government bonds had been passive. In other words, both in the first and second increase of the income tax, no steps were taken to increase the rates on Class II incomes. But positive steps to favor government bonds were taken in 1905, and again in 1909, when they were expressly exempted from income taxation. The law enacted in February, 1905, exempted from income tax the interest on all government bonds issued after 1904 for military purposes. The second step in this direction was taken in March, 1909, when interest on all government bonds, without regard to kind, was exempted by law from the income tax.

The emergency special tax law was to be abolished at the close of the Russo-Japanese War, but this did not materialize because the disposition of post-bellum affairs required a large amount of government expenditure. Although the tax system was revised twice, in 1908 and again in 1910, the method of levying income tax was left without needed adjustments until 1913, when the law was revised and the Emergency Law was abolished *in toto*.

THE THIRD PERIOD, 1913-1920

REVISIONS OF INCOME TAX

Revision of 1913. After the thorough revision of 1899 no substantial improvement was made, except minor revisions, because the emergency special tax law remained in force for many years, even after the close of the Russo-Japanese war. A fundamental and lasting revision was greatly needed to provide for an adjustment between corporate income and individual income. A bill for revising the income tax law was presented by Finance Minister Korekiyo Takahashi to the 30th session of the Imperial Diet in 1913 side by side with a bill for abolishing the emergency special tax law. It was modified by the House of Representatives and the revised bill was accepted by the House of Peers, becoming a law in the same year.

The features of revision of 1913 may be summarized as follows:

The structure and rates of the income tax were revised. Income A in Class I was changed to B in the same class. As to the rates, simple progressive rates were replaced by an excess progressive rate applied to income A in Class I, and to Class III. For small individual incomes reductions of fixed amounts were granted in indirect progression. The number of brackets of progression were increased for all individual incomes. These two revisions were great improvements in Japan's taxation system.

The exemption point which had remained at 300 yen was raised to 400 yen. Adjustment was made in the method of calculating individual incomes, although the underlying principle of estimation, as determined in 1899, remained. A fixed deduction was allowed for earned income, the first instance of the kind in Japan. Income accruing from essential industries during a certain fixed period of time was exempted. The obligation to make a declaration to the revenue office was extended to third persons.

Revision of 1918. World War I broke out in 1914, and Japan was forced into it at an early stage. Her financial circle was confronted with unprecedented events such as soaring prices, a business boom, and a large expansion of government expenditures. The need was felt for adjusting the income tax law to the prevailing financial condition and at the same time, the War Department made plans to build up the military forces, while the Navy Department contemplated expanding the naval program. The government presented a bill for revising the income tax law in March, 1918. This bill was explained by Finance Minister Shoda substantially as follows:

The principal aim of the bill is to raise the rates of income tax for both corporate and individual incomes by 20 percent. The tax rate on the interest on debentures is to be raised by 1 percent. The exemption point for Class III incomes was raised from 400 to 500 yen. We have given some consideration to reduction from incomes under 1,000 yen. Another feature in the bill is that we have provided an extra bracket above the highest of progressive brackets for both corporate and individual incomes. The government has accepted minor revisions made in the bill by the House of Representatives.

The House of Peers sanctioned the revisions and the bill became law. The 1918 revision was only partial. It had two important features. In the first place, the tax rates were raised. On the incomes of joint-stock companies a proportional income tax of 7.5 percent was levied. Rates were differentiated for interest on government bonds and interest on debentures. For individual income, a new bracket of 200,000 yen was newly created and excess progressive rates ranging from 3 percent to 30 percent were levied. The amount of reductions for small incomes was increased. Secondly, the exemption point for Class III was raised to 500 yen.

THE FOURTH PERIOD, 1920-1940
EFFORTS AT MODERNIZATION

Aggregate income taxation against withholding-at-source taxation. Whereas the income tax law of 1887 was merely a copy of the Western system, the income tax system of 1899, which had become the basis of the income tax law for a long time, was a sort of classified income tax. The original draft of the income tax presented to the 12th session of the Diet was a five-class progressive income tax: it was a compromise between the withholding-at-source income tax and the aggregate income tax. But this tax draft, as referred to before, was not enacted into law because the Diet was dissolved. The government income tax bill presented to the 13th session of the Diet was a three-class income tax. Although it was modified to a two-class income tax by the House of Representatives, it was changed back to the three-class income tax of the original bill by the House of Peers. It was characteristic of our income tax law, as emphasized by the government delegate, Mr. Wakatsuki, that corporate income (Class I) and interest on capital (Class II) were to be taxed at the source, while Class III incomes were to be taxed on the aggregate sum of incomes at the place where taxpayers receive them. This view, however, brought out a controversial issue in the academic world of Japan. Dr. Gotaro Ogawa, Professor of Kyoto Imperial University, was most vehement in criticizing that very point, as objectionable policy. On two occasions, in 1915 and 1920, Dr. Ogawa in his lecture on "The Social Policy Society" of Japan criticized the 1899 income tax law substantially as follows:

In our revenue taxes, the income tax lies in the center; there are also the land tax levied on real estate and the business tax levied on business transactions. Since business represents the activity of capital and labor combined, capital which is not used for business must also be taxed. Liquid assets, in most cases, take the form of negotiable securities of which the principal ones are government bonds, debentures, and shares. Let us see how our income tax deals with these securities. First, take bonds and debentures. Income from these is classified as Class II income on which a 2 percent tax is levied, irrespective of amount. For instance a taxpayer who receives an income of as much as 10 thousand yen from such bonds and debentures will pay a tax of only 2 percent of his income. The owners of land are taxed twice: they have to pay the income tax as well as the land tax. Business men also are taxed twice: they have to pay the income tax as well as the business tax. But the owners of bonds and debentures will be taxed only once, and the rate of the tax is only 2 percent. Moreover, no tax is levied on government bonds at all. This policy, which has been enforced since the time of the Katsura Cabinet, is open to serious criticism.

I shall now take up the tax on dividends from shares. No tax is levied on the corporate dividend. It is merely levied on the net income of joint-stock companies. Our lawmakers have explained this by saying that it is too troublesome to tax the individual dividend after it has been paid out, and that it would be convenient to tax it while it is still in the hands of joint-stock companies. Now joint-stock companies in our country regard income tax as a sort of business expense and they do not deduct the tax from the amount of dividend, and companies with a sound financial basis attempt to maintain a definite rate of dividend. They make no attempt to shift the burden of income tax to the shareholders even when the rate of the tax has been increased. Thus, our shareholders do not have the feeling that they are shouldering the tax burden as far as the dividend they secure is concerned. We may truly say that the dividend on shares is exempted from income tax. Even supposing that the taxation of corporate income is a convenient method of taxing dividends, the fact remains that the tax is proportional and no progressive tax is levied on such income.

With the advance of society, the amount of bonds, debentures, and shares will be increased and they will represent the wealth of the property class. But the tax on these at present is very light. Their taxation is not harmonious with social policy.

Again, in his work "Our Public Finance from the Viewpoint of Social Policy," Dr. Ogawa argues:

It is well that the income tax in force adopts progressive taxation, but its rates are very heavy for individual income and light for partnerships and joint partnerships. As to the income of joint-stock companies, no progressive tax is levied thereon, it being subject to a proportional tax only. We may say that the greater the capital the lighter the tax imposed. Individual income is supposed to be taxed properly but in reality it fails to catch the greater part of the national income inasmuch as income derived from interest on bonds and debentures, and from dividends and bonuses, is not taxed. Of course one may say that the gains from these negotiable securities are indirectly taxed as corporate income or as Class II income. But the former is usually deducted as a business expense and does not affect dividends, and for this reason it can be said that the dividends paid to individuals are free from all taxes. As to the latter, it must be remembered that government bonds are exempted from income tax. If we tax joint-stock companies lightly and exempt negotiable securities or tax them lightly, the rich will become richer, and discontent over the unjust system of tax distribution will be intensified.

The reaction took the form of a movement in favor of the imposition of an aggregate income tax on corporate income (Class I) and on interest on capital (Class II), thereby replacing the withholding-at-source system. At this very juncture, there was a trend in other countries to adopt an aggregate income tax, or a surtax on income, in addition to the classified income tax or the usual income tax hitherto adopted, and this trend assisted very materially our movement in favor of the aggregate form of income tax.

Bill presented in the 42d session of the Diet. Although World War I had ushered in an unexpected prosperity in the economic activity of Japan, it also gave rise to an undesirable phenomenon in the distribution of wealth. In 1919 or thereabouts considerable social discontent was manifested in a political movement for universal franchise. It was at that time, that is to say, during the 42d session of the Diet, that Premier Takashi Hara introduced a new income tax bill.

The revision made by this bill of Japan's income tax law was epoch-making, inasmuch as the traditional withholding-at-source system was replaced by an aggregate income system, except in regard to Class II. On this point a debate occurred between Finance Minister Takahashi and Dr. Gotaro Ogawa, who said to the Finance Minister:

I wish to ask questions about the substance of the income tax law now before the House. The law has abolished the withholding-at-source system as regards Class I income, or corporate income. I believe this is a great improvement in our tax system, and I heartily support it. But I should like to hear the government's reason for abolishing this system.

To this Finance Minister Takahashi replied, in substance:

The government abolished the withholding-at-source system because it is unjust for individual taxpayers. Under this system, persons whose income is 1 hundred yen will have to pay the same rate of tax as persons whose income is several million yen. That will be unjust to tax payers. The government abolished the withholding-at-source system because it believes that the personal taxation of aggregate income is in conformity with justice.

The bill was modified in minor details by the House of Representatives. One of the modifications was a deduction of 20 percent of the income individuals receive from corporations. In the House of Peers, Finance Minister Takahashi explained that this modification was made by the House of Representatives because of its fear that taxing individuals on income from dividends might jeopardize the development of industry.

This bill failed to become law because the House of Representatives was dissolved on February 26, before the House of Peers could complete its deliberation of the bill. The bill bore special significance for the reason that, whereas the only object of revisions of the income tax law previously attempted was to secure revenue for the government, this bill had some social-political aspect in view.

The law of 1920. Under the law of 1920, an aggregate income tax was levied on 60 percent of the corporate dividends and bonuses of individuals.

The corporate income tax (Class I) was divided into five parts: a reserve income tax on income held in reserve by a corporation instead of being paid out as dividends; the dividend income tax on corporate income paid out as dividends; the liquidation income tax for a surplus when liquidated; excess income tax for income exceeding 10 percent of the operating capital; and income tax for foreign corporations.

The structure of Class II income was retained and interest on time deposits at banks was added to it, while the rates on interest on bonds and debentures were raised.

Various improvements were made in regard to Class III income.

The principle of aggregate income taxation was more thoroughly applied, and not only dividends and bonuses received from corporations but also bonuses received from the government and other public organizations, as well as income received in territories outside the jurisdiction of the income tax law, all these consolidated incomes were taxed. The exemption point was raised to 800 yen and tax rates were revised. The method of taxing income from forestry was changed.

The assessment of, and the reductions from, earned income were improved. A special reduction was provided for the first time in Japan for each dependent.

Revision of 1926. Between 1920 and 1926 there were numerous minor changes in the law. In 1922 interest on money in trust was included as taxable. In 1923 all bank deposits were included, instead of time deposits only, as had been the case hitherto, and the income tax investigation commission was authorized to regard as dividend all reserves exceeding a certain limit. A maximum reduction of 200 yen was provided for a life insurance premium paid on an insurance policy of which the beneficiary was the taxpayer or a member of his family or his heir.

Major revisions were made in 1926 in regard to corporate income. The bill for effecting these revisions was introduced during the 50th session of the Diet together with other bills for the adjustment of the tax system. The substance of the bill was, in effect, explained as follows by Finance Minister Yuko Hamaguchi.

The proposed bill will abolish the progressive taxation on the reserve income of corporations. By eliminating the distinction between the reserve income and the dividend income a proportional tax of 5 percent on the total amount of corporate incomes is levied. Under the present income tax law, a proportional tax of 5 percent is levied on the dividend income while a progressive tax of from 5 percent to 20 percent is levied on the reserve income. As a result of this distinction between the two forms of income, corporations tend to keep reserves as small as possible in order to incur the least tax burden, and this, in turn, tends to weaken the financial status of corporations and jeopardize industrial development in general. The income tax now in force is originally intended to prevent undue reservation of income by corporations, to evade the aggregated tax on dividends, but as it is applied indiscriminately to all corporations, it results, in actual cases, in an undue taxation on law-abiding corporations, and does not suit the actual circumstances. The bill before the House proposes to abolish the progressive taxation of the reserve income, to do away with the existing distinction between the dividend and reserve incomes, and to levy a proportional tax of 5 percent on the total corporate income. The government is quite mindful of the possibility of tax evasion by family corporations carrying unduly large reserves, but it is desirous of revising the law in order to assure justice in taxation.

We have decided to deduct from Class I income the amount of the Class II income tax paid during the business year, in order to prevent double taxation on Class I and Class II incomes.

We intend to raise the exemption point of Class III income from 800 yen to 1,200 yen.

The tax on income from forestry is calculated by multiplying the amount of the tax by five, on one-fifth of the income.

A deduction of 100 yen is to be made for each dependant supported by taxpayers whose incomes are below 3,000 yen per year.

There was a heated debate before the bill was finally passed by the two Houses of the Diet in its original form and became law in March, 1926.

The structure and rates of Class I income were changed. The progressive taxation on corporate reserve income was abolished, and laws regarding family corporations were revised in order to prevent evasion of the income tax. The distinction between dividend and reserve incomes was abolished, and a proportional tax of 5 percent was provided for the ordinary incomes of corporations. The amount of Class II income tax paid during the business year became deductible from Class I income, in order to prevent double taxation on these. The rates for liquidation income and the income of foreign corporations were modified.

The tax on Class III income was changed as to the exemption point and deductions for family members dependent on taxpayers for support and for earned income. The method of calculating corporate income was changed from "the estimated total income from which necessary expenses have been deducted" to "the total income of the previous year, from which necessary expenses have been deducted." The method of calculating income from forestry was also changed.

Revisions after 1935. The Manchuria struggle in 1931 brought about the expansion of public expenditures, thereby terminating the stabilization of public finance which had lasted from 1926 to 1935 and necessitating a fundamental tax reform. In 1935, the extraordinary profit tax law was enacted; imposing a tax on the excess income over the average business profit. This law was in force until 1946. Mr. Baba, the Finance Minister of the Hirota Cabinet, attempted a far-reaching tax reform of both national and local taxes but it was turned down by the Diet as too radical. Mr. Yuki, Finance Minister of the Hayashi Cabinet, managed to put through the Temporary Tax Increment Law (Law No. 3 March 30, 1937), which increased the rates all around on the incomes of Classes I, II, and III. Following this, Mr. Kaya, the Finance Minister of the Konoe Cabinet, drafted the North China Incident Special Tax Law (Law No. 66 August 12, 1937) which again raised the rates of income tax. As the North China struggle continued and spread, the China Affair Special Tax (Law No. 51 March 31, 1938) took the place of the earlier North China Incident Special Tax.

THE FIFTH PERIOD, 1940 TO 1945, ESTABLISHMENT OF A MODERN SYSTEM

Structural revision of 1940. A fundamental revision of the tax system had been pending since Dr. Baba's failure in 1937. As the North China struggle spread, demanding more and more expenditures, Mr. Sakurauchi, Finance Minister of the Yonai Cabinet, introduced fundamental reform of the national and local taxation system in the course of the 75th session of the Diet. Transitional legislation such as the China Affair Special Tax Law, the Temporary Tax Increment Law, and the Corporation's Capital Tax Law were abolished as a matter of course.

As a result of the reform, the old income tax system of three classes was abolished and two income tax classes were established; they were the corporation income tax and the individual income tax. The former took the place of the old corporation income tax Class I, and the latter took the place of old Class II and Class III.

The distinction between individual income tax and corporate income tax was of a pattern followed in the United States and Germany, and the distinction between the classified tax and the aggregate tax was adopted from the English and French systems. The intention was to adopt all advanced systems of other countries.

The classified income tax, the nucleus of direct taxes, was imposed on incomes in six groups: real estate, dividends and interest, enterprises, labor services, forestry enterprises, and retirement allowance incomes, with proportionate rates. Provisions were made for the exemption point, basic exemption, dependency credit, and reduction for life insurance premiums.

The rates of tax were as follows: on income from real estate, 10 percent; from dividends and interest, 10 percent; Class A, on national bonds, 4 percent; local bonds, 9 percent; others, 10 percent and Class B, 10 percent; from enterprise, Class A, 8.5 percent and Class B, 7.5 percent; from labor service, 6 percent; from forestry, under 1,600 yen, 5 percent; over 1,600 yen, 7.5 percent; from retirement allowances under 20,000 yen, 6 percent; over 20,000 yen, 12 percent; over 100,000 yen, 25 percent; over 500,000 yen, 40 percent.

The aggregate income tax was imposed on individual aggregated incomes at progressive rates: over 5,000 yen, 10 percent; over 8,000 yen, 15 percent; over 12,000 yen, 20 percent; over 20,000 yen, 25 percent; over 30,000 yen, 30 percent; over 50,000 yen, 35 percent; over 80,000 yen, 40 percent; over 120,000 yen, 45 percent; over 200,000 yen, 50 percent; over 300,000 yen, 55 percent; over 500,000 yen, 60 percent; over 800,000 yen, 65 percent.

For corporations, the corporation tax was levied on normal income, liquidation and capital incomes during the fiscal year. At the same time, the Special Corporation Tax Law was enacted. Under this law normal business incomes accrued during the fiscal year of corporations having the head office or principal places of business within the area where the corporation tax law was enforced, the rate was 18 percent. For corporations not having the head office or principal places of business within the enforcement area of the corporation tax law the rate was 28 percent. The rate on income from liquidation was set at 18 percent and that on capital at 0.15 percent.

Revision of 1942. As against the revision of 1941 (August), effected immediately before World War II to deal with indirect taxes, the revision of 1942 principally affected direct taxes. The increase of rates was fairly high on all these (classified income, aggregate income, and corporate taxes), but that of the classified income tax was most prominent. The changes in this case aimed at an increase of 60 percent of the total revenue by raising rates and lowering various deductions, giving due consideration to the matter of fair distribution of tax among different classes of incomes. Dependency credit and deduction for life insurance premiums were favorably treated.

Regarding the aggregate income tax, the revision sought a net 30 percent increase of the total revenue by lowering the minimum taxable income.

As to the corporation tax, the rates were raised from 18 percent to

25 percent for normal corporate income and from 6 percent to 12.5 percent for special corporate income.

Revision of 1944. This was another attempt to increase revenue to meet expanded military expenses and others. It affected both direct and indirect taxes and served to simplify the taxation system.

Features worth mentioning in the revision of income taxes were the removal of forestry income from the categories of the aggregate incomes, the change of rates of the classified incomes, and the reduction of the number of installments of tax payments to twice a year for small taxpayers.

The classified income tax was expected to increase tax revenue by 50 percent through an extension of the scope of assessment as well as an upward revision of the rates. The rates of the aggregate income tax were also raised to produce an 18 percent increase in revenue. The rates were also raised on the corporation tax and the special corporation tax.

Revision of 1945. With the adverse developments of the war situation during 1944, Japan's defeat seemed inevitable. The shortage of materials was so acute that production declined alarmingly. In the financial phase, the bottom of taxable sources had been reached, and two attempts to increase revenue resulted in simplifying the tax system rather than in raising the rates.

The first revision (April) was principally confined to the classified income tax, the rate of which was increased by 3 percent to produce a 20 percent increase of revenue; the tax became payable twice a year. The rates of corporation tax and special corporation tax were also increased. Particular attention should be called to the fact that the partial adoption of the self-assessment system was adopted for the corporation tax for those corporations with a capital of over 5 million yen, and this should be considered as the forerunner of the new postwar taxation system.

The second revision was made when the mainlands were already exposed to open attack. It was made effective by Ordinance No. 423, issued on July 21, without the Diet's sanction as it was impossible to go through the normal procedure. Incidentally this was the final revision made during the war. Japan surrendered on August 15, 1945.

The revision was effected at a time when the nation's economy was in a state of complete confusion. Little could be expected out of it, under the circumstances, and the simplification of the taxation system was about all it could produce. One feature which deserved attention was the adoption of the system of assessment on estimated incomes for the current year to deal with the vastly increased income of the war rich, cementing a foundation for the widely practiced self-assessment system which was to come after the war.

THE SIXTH PERIOD, 1946-1950 REORGANIZATION

Revision of income and corporation taxes in 1946. The unconditional surrender on August 15, 1945, was followed by the Allied occupation of the country, and all policies were carried out in conformity with the provisions laid down in the Potsdam Declaration. Of the four revisions effected in 1946, three concerned income tax.

Along with the first official commodity prices fixed after the war, the income tax was revised in March, 1946. Concerning the classified income tax, the basic exemption for forestry income was raised from 400 yen to 1,200 yen. The basic exemption for Class A of earned income was raised from 600 yen to 2,400 yen, and dependency credit was raised from 24 yen to 72 yen. The taxable minimum of the aggregate income tax was raised from 3,000 yen to 10,000 yen.

The second revision was carried out in September. In order to simplify the taxation system, the extraordinary profit tax was merged into the corporate tax and income tax. In the field of the classified income tax, the rate on property income was raised by 25 percent to fall in with the policy of levying a heavier tax on properties and in line with that policy, the classified income tax was imposed on income arising out of transfer of fixed assets (capital gain).

The outstanding feature in the third revision of the year (December) was the creation of the increased-income tax. As a result of the practice of assessment on an estimate of the current year's income (first adopted partially in July, 1945) there became evident a wide discrepancy between the actual tax amount of the previous year and the estimated tax of the current year. The increased-income tax was designed in the light of this discrepancy by levying a tax on the advance in the current year over the actual income of the previous year.

Revision of 1947. The promulgation of the new Constitution in November, 1946 ushered in a new era and firmly established the foundation of democratic Japan. The existing taxation system was, after all, a war time improvisation. There was now a natural demand for fundamental and structural revision to suit the democratized society. The reform of 1947 was an adaptation of the American system. It was passed by the 92d session of the Diet, which, incidentally, was the last session under the old Constitution. Eliminating the distinction between the classified income and the aggregate income, the progressive tax rate was applied to the consolidated individual incomes. The self-assessment system for the current year was used for all incomes, doing away with the old method of assessment for the preceding year. The basic deduction of 4,800 yen, the 20 percent deduction for earned income, the dependency credit of 240 yen per person and rates ranging from 20 percent to 75 percent were provided for. The tax on earned income, dividend, and interest, was collected at the source, subject to adjustment at the time of final return.

The corporation tax was also revised after the American model. The tax rates for excess income and capital were revised, and the self-assessment system was enlarged to include all corporations, declarations to be made within two months after the close of the fiscal business year with the tax payable at the same time.

The second revision of 1947 (December) was made effective by the 1st session of the Diet summoned under the new Constitution. In spite of strenuous efforts there was no sign of a termination of the vicious cycle of prices and wages. The government, therefore, tried to stabilize wages by a considerable rise in official commodity prices, necessitating another revision of tax within the same year to make up the deficiency of the budget. In the income tax the reduction for earned income was raised to 25 percent and the dependency credit to 360 yen per person, to parallel the advance in commodity prices. The rate for high incomes was also increased so as to equalize the tax burden between the general public and the war rich. The rise in rates of the family corporation tax was intended to adjust corporation income tax to individual income tax.

Revision of 1948. At the beginning of 1948, there appeared signs in the occupation policy of a move toward the economic independence of Japan. The tax revision of that year affected indirect taxes in proportion to the rise in prices and wages. On the other hand, measures were taken to relieve the burden of the heavy income tax, and also the corporation tax was reduced to stimulate industries and to invite foreign capital. The revised income tax included a rise in the basic exemption to 15,000 yen and in the dependency credit to 1,800 yen per person; a revision of the brackets and rates ranging from 20 percent to 80 percent;

and a deduction of 15 percent for dividend income; the rates for foreign corporations and individuals were made the same as those for domestic corporations and individuals.

The corporation tax was affected by the abolition of the special corporation tax through merging the pertinent regulations with the corporation tax law; the abolition of the tax on capital; the lowering of the tax rate on excess income; and the bringing of the tax rate on ordinary income of foreign corporations to the level of domestic corporations.

THE SEVENTH PERIOD, 1950 TO 1955, THE SHOUP RECOMMENDATIONS

The outstanding feature of the Shoup Recommendations was to treat the income tax as the nucleus of the tax system, lessening the role of circulation taxes and consumption taxes. According to Dr. Shoup's ideal, in ten years' time, the income tax, both national and local, would reach the desired goal of 75 percent of the entire tax revenue.

Income tax reform of 1950. The new income tax law offered two special features: self-assessment and assessment on estimates of the current year's income. The idea of self-assessment had been advanced when the classified and the aggregate income taxes were united in 1947. Assessment on estimates of current income was initiated for part of the tax in 1945, but in 1947, it was more widely adopted. The reform of 1950 perfected these two features. Other changes were an increase in (1) the basic exemption and in (2) dependency credit, a special deduction for (3) disability, (4) disaster, and (5) medical expenses. On (6) the deduction of earned income, the maximum amount was narrowed and the rate for each bracket was set as follows: up to 50,000 yen, 20 percent; over 50,000 yen and up to 80,000 yen, 25 percent; over 80,000 yen up to 100,000 yen, 30 percent; over 100,000 yen up to 120,000 yen, 35 percent; over 120,000 yen up to 150,000 yen, 40 percent; over 150,000 yen up to 200,000 yen, 45 percent; over 200,000 yen up to 500,000 yen, 50 percent; and over 500,000 yen, 55 percent.

The maximum rate was kept fairly low to encourage production and also because the deficit could be made up by the creation of (7) the net-worth tax, and raising the maximum rate of (8) the accession tax.

The allowable period during which (9) profit and loss could be adjusted was extended so that loss could be carried over for a longer period; the creation of a new system allowing carry-back of loss was worth mentioning.

On (10) fluctuating incomes, the taxpayer could use the method of (11) average taxation if more than 25 percent of his total income came from (12) fishery rights, (13) manuscript or music rights, (14) copyrights, (15) retiring allowances, (16) forestry rights, or (17) capital gains.

The original cost of a capital gain or forestry income was multiplied by a figure set by (18) the fixed-assets revaluation law in order to compute (19) the acquisition cost. This was to eliminate gains or losses caused merely by a change in the value of money.

As for (20) income from dividends, the sum equivalent to 25 percent of the dividend received was deducted from the tax amount calculated for the total income including dividends. This subject will later be touched upon in the next section, which deals with the corporation tax.

Corporation tax reform of 1950. The adjustment of double taxation on individual and corporation incomes by the provision of the income tax law and the free adoption of modern ideas of accounting must be cited as noteworthy features of the new corporation tax law.

The question of double taxation on individual and corporation has a historical record. It was originally presented to the Diet in 1898 by Mr. R. Wakatsuki; later, in 1915 and 1920, it was presented by Dr. Ogawa at the meetings of the Social Policy Society, and ever since it had been a controversial subject in academic circles. It was once solved after the German theory in 1940, and ten years later a completely novel interpretation was given by the Shoup Recommendations in 1950.

Prior to the reform, the law had treated a corporation as an independent taxpayer, levying a tax on its income on the one hand, and on the other hand, charging an individual income tax on dividend which was a part of corporation income. The Shoup Mission regarded a corporation as a group of individuals rather than as an independent entity, and the reform was made according to this interpretation. Inasmuch as corporations pay the corporation tax, the tax on dividends should be decreased by that amount. However, a new tax was created on reserves not distributed as dividends. The (21) excess-profits tax on corporations was abolished and the (22) liquidation income tax was also withdrawn.

Reserves were made taxable at the rate of 2 percent for a (23) ordinary corporation and 7 percent for a (24) family corporation.

Dividends received from other corporations were excluded from a corporation profit; the period during which loss could be carried over was extended to five years and a new system of allowing loss to be carried back and deducted from the previous year's profit was established; modern accounting theory was introduced into (25) the method of inventory valuation, (26) depreciation of fixed assets, and also of making distinction between expenses for (27) repairing, and (28) capital disbursements.

Reform of 1951. By the reform of 1950, the income tax and the corporation tax were so drastically remodeled that certain minor revisions were necessary to make it function smoothly. These revisions legislated twice in 1951, at the ordinary session and the extraordinary session of the Diet, were of the following nature.

As to the income tax, the assessment standard was rationalized in several ways. Increases were made in the basic exemption, dependency credit, and the reduction for disability, and also by providing reductions for (29) old age, (30) widows, (31) student's earned incomes, and (32) life insurance premiums. The withholding method was placed at the taxpayer's option for (33) interest on deposits and savings, at the rate of 50 percent. The brackets were expanded at the following rates: under 80,000 yen, 20 percent; over 80,000 yen, 25 percent; over 120,000 yen, 30 percent; over 200,000 yen, 35 percent; over 300,000 yen, 40 percent; over 500,000 yen, 45 percent, over 1 million yen, 50 percent; over 2 million yen, 55 percent.

Income from retirement allowances was treated differently from other incomes in that a special reduction of 150,000 yen was allowed and the ordinary rate was applied for half the balance. This step was taken to provide a sort of social security that was needed in a country where governmental measures of the kind are still backward and the retirement allowance is regarded more or less as back payment of salaries. For the income from dividends, the rate of 20 percent was applied on the withholding basis and the amount thus withheld could be deducted from the tax return in addition to the regular deduction for dividends.

The corporation tax was also revised in various aspects. The corporation tax on reserves was abolished except for the rate of 5 percent on family corporations. The purpose was to correct unhealthy management operating chiefly on borrowed money, and to restore sound finance of corporations by the accumulation of capital. The rate for corporation income was advanced from 35 percent to 42 percent.

In order to speed up modernization of essential industries, special depreciation was allowed for certain new machinery or equipment.

The reserve for price depreciation to the extent of 10 percent for inventories and shares and 5 percent for debentures and local bonds was admitted. It aimed at providing a cushion for frequent and violent price-fluctuation of current assets due to the unsteady economic condition of Japan. The legal status of reserve funds for retirement allowances which corporations had been allowed to include in loss was defined.

The income tax and the corporation tax were revised every year from 1950 to 1955. The following is the present income and corporation tax law, in comparison with that of 1950 which was proclaimed to implement the tax reform of Dr. Shoup's.

The aggregate income taxation method was modified in respect to income from interest, from retirement, and from forestry. The tax on capital gain of securities was repealed to be replaced by the securities transaction tax. The basic exemption was increased from 25,000 yen to 80,000 yen. For earned incomes, the maximum deduction was increased from 30,000 yen to 60,000 yen. Dependency credit was raised from 12,000 yen to 40,000 yen for the first dependent, 25,000 yen each for the second and third, and 15,000 yen for each of the rest. The disability tax reduction was fixed at 5,000 yen. A certain exemption was allowed to the aged, to widows, and to working students. The provisions in regard to accidents remained unchanged but reductions for insurance premiums and social insurance premiums were added. As for the tax rates, the present structure has eleven brackets with progressive rates ranging from 15 percent on incomes less than 30,000 yen to 65 percent on more than 5 million yen, in comparison with the eight brackets and progressive rates from 20 percent on less than 50,000 yen to 55 percent on more than 500,000 yen in 1950. The 15 percent of dividend incomes and the 10 percent of interest incomes are withheld at sources. Interest incomes are not included in aggregate incomes. Interest income due on and after the first of July, 1955, until March, 1957, is exempt from the income tax. The dividend reduction rate of 25 percent was raised to 30 percent. The revisions of the corporation tax were less complicated. The tax rate for the income of corporations is 35 percent on income less than 500,000 yen and 40 percent on the part of income exceeding 500,000 yen and that of special corporations is 35 percent. The taxation on liquidation income was established. The taxation on reserves of corporations other than family corporations was

TABLE 24

PERCENTAGE OF INCOME TAX TO MAJOR TAXES AND MONOPOLY REVENUE COMBINED, 1889–1939

(In thousand yen)

	Major Tax Revenue						
Year	*Land Tax*	*Income Tax*	*Liquor Tax*	*Customs Duties*	*Monopoly Revenue*	*Total*	*Percentage of Income Tax to Other Taxes and Monopoly Revenue*
1889	42,161	1,052	16,439	4,728		71,294	1.48
1890	40,084	1,092	13,912	4,392		66,114	1.65
1891	37,457	1,110	14,686	4,539		64,423	1.72
1892	37,925	1,132	15,812	4,991		67,167	1.69
1893	38,808	1,283	16,637	5,125		70,004	1.83
1894	39,291	1,353	16,130	5,755		71,286	1.90
1895	38,692	1,497	17,748	6,785		74,697	2.00
1896	37,640	1,810	19,476	6,728		76,387	2.37
1897	37,964	2,095	31,105	8,020		94,912	2.21
1898	38,440	2,351	32,959	9,092		97,629	2.41
1899	44,861	4,837	48,918	15,936		126,034	3.84
1900	46,717	6,368	50,293	17,009	7,244	141,170	4.51
1901	46,666	6,836	58,017	13,630	10,866	150,441	4.54
1902	46,505	7,460	63,738	15,501	12,367	163,452	4.56
1903	46,873	8,247	52,821	17,378	14,898	161,061	5.12
1904	60,939	14,369	58,286	23,159	27,462	221,824	6.48
1905	80,473	23,278	59,099	36,757	33,602	284,877	8.17
1906	84,637	26,348	71,100	41,853	32,574	316,043	8.34
1907	84,973	27,291	78,406	50,027	35,607	351,591	7.76
1908	85,418	32,144	83,590	40,067	61,419	384,055	8.37
1909	85,693	32,800	91,480	36,423	58,449	381,856	8.59
1910	76,291	31,722	86,701	39,949	62,089	379,375	8.36

1911	74,936	34,755	86,032	48,518	63,336	392,407	8.86
1912	75,365	38,933	93,861	68,496	66,015	426,985	9.12
1913	74,635	35,591	93,223	73,722	69,297	438,777	8.11
1914	74,925	37,157	95,781	44,228	54,587	398,296	9.33
1915	73,602	37,567	84,649	32,165	68,803	381,548	9.85
1916	73,274	51,284	89,837	35,918	67,127	415,800	12.33
1917	73,478	94,649	106,738	45,186	77,592	508,196	18.62
1918	73,527	122,817	120,635	68,937	89,515	608,808	20.17
1919	73,754	193,148	137,626	81,135	74,467	746,853	25.86
1920	73,944	190,344	163,896	69,371	124,124	820,381	23.20
1921	74,130	200,938	176,085	100,941	124,289	910,141	22.08
1922	74,325	229,132	222,585	108,044	129,670	1,026,074	22.33
1923	73,134	163,846	221,497	89,309	130,157	917,360	17.86
1924	71,969	209,992	221,577	119,638	148,231	1,035,469	20.28
1925	74,614	234,971	212,638	111,160	153,029	1,047,837	22.42
1926	68,728	209,577	216,583	150,612	167,403	1,054,402	19.88
1927	67,576	215,070	242,037	140,600	173,257	1,071,931	20.06
1928	67,821	206,741	235,749	150,944	177,201	1,093,111	18.91
1929	67,484	199,851	242,562	136,096	177,803	1,071,308	18.65
1930	68,262	204,955	220,601	105,504	198,339	1,033,380	19.83
1931	64,391	147,604	190,190	114,562	190,461	925,965	15.94
1932	58,764	139,329	179,145	105,661	177,906	873,743	15.94
1933	58,459	162,335	209,366	114,390	179,266	926,606	17.52
1934	57,916	198,568	219,152	145,444	192,571	1,093,760	18.15
1935	58,229	230,378	209,845	151,374	197,562	1,188,586	19.38
1936	58,738	278,631	220,572	174,612	215,166	1,327,067	20.99
1937	58,555	482,510	242,277	185,131	257,586	1,812,873	26.61
1938	51,612	735,412	278,831	166,591	261,307	2,344,055	31.37
1939	48,718	892,704	266,836	148,795	320,219	2,917,385	30.59

repealed. For family corporations, a 10 percent tax is imposed on the newly accumulated part of reserve over one million yen or 25 percent of the capital, whichever is larger.

REVIEW OF THE DEVELOPMENT OF THE INCOME TAX

As has been explained, the income tax law in Japan has passed through seven stages. The first stage may be described as a period of imitation, importing foreign systems for experimental purposes. It is evident that the laws of that era were strongly influenced by foreign systems through foreign financial advisers. It was only during the second period that an income tax law adaptable to our national environment came into existence, and some of its essentials remained in force until as late as 1920. During the second period, the Russo-Japanese War necessitated an increase in revenue, and a temporary revision of the income tax law was effected; but it was not until the third period that a thorough-going revision was contemplated. Shortly after the third period started, World War I broke out and the income tax came to occupy a very important position in tax revenues. The necessity for embodying social and economic considerations in the law was responsible for the fundamental revision made during the fourth period. The revision of the fifth period transferred the tax on Class A income to the corporation tax, and the income tax was divided into classified income and aggregate income. This modern system was no doubt partly influenced by European models, but it was introduced mainly on the initiative of the Japanese and has grown in Japanese soil. The period of World War II witnessed many revisions in income and corporation tax laws. In the sixth period, a number of emergency measures were enforced in conformity with the occupation policy in the aftermath of the war. The seventh period was marked by the revolutionary reform recommended by the Shoup Mission.

Thus our income tax has developed from its crude form of 1887 to the fairly complex and very modern form of today. Its future development will, of course, depend on the future state of affairs, but it may not be difficult to forecast the general course on the basis of past performance.

Income tax revenue compared with major taxes and monopoly revenues. An interesting fact is discovered when the income tax is compared with other major national taxes such as the land tax, the liquor tax and customs duties, and the revenue from government monopolies. Table 24 gives these figures for 50 years, 1889 to 1939.

The tax revenue of the first period was largely made up of the tax on land and liquor, and the income tax was less than the customs duties, between 1.48 percent and 2.41 percent of total major tax revenue. In the second period, the revenue from government monopolies was added. While it yielded more than the income tax revenue, the land and liquor taxes still predominated. But the income tax revenue increased from 3.84 percent to 9.12 percent of all revenues during the period.

Conditions at the beginning of the third period were substantially the same as those in the second period, but with the outbreak of World War I, the revenue from the income tax greatly increased and in 1919 it constituted 25.86 percent of the total, heading the list of revenues, with the tax on liquor second, and customs duties third, followed by the revenue from monopolies and the land tax. In the early part of the fourth period, the income tax revenue still held first place, but in the post-war depression it took a downward trend, while government income from the land tax, the tax on liquor, customs duties, and revenue from monopolies maintained their high positions as during the war. From 1933 onward, the percentage of the income tax rose to the top once more, followed by the monopoly revenue, the liquor tax, customs duties, and the land tax in last place. The percentage of the income tax stood at 30.59 percent in 1939.

Table 25 brings the comparison up to 1955.

It reveals that the income tax and corporation tax combined represented 39.64 percent of the total major taxes and the monopoly revenue in 1940 and 50.99 percent in 1955. It can be summed up from the foregoing that our income tax steadily developed over the past sixty-odd years until it became foremost of the direct taxes.

CONCLUSION

The following list gives a chronological record of the adoption of a national income tax by different countries. The results of the investigation made by Popitz (Johannes Popitz: Einkommensteuer *Handworterbuch der Staatswissenschaften,* 4th ed., Vol. III, secs. 437-91) are quoted, with some necessary revisions: 1798, Great Britain; 1840, Switzerland; 1862, United States; 1864, Italy; 1884, Serbia and South Australia; 1887, Japan; 1891, New Zealand; 1893, Holland; 1894, Tas-

TABLE 25

PERCENTAGE OF INCOME AND CORPORATION TAXES TO MAJOR TAXES AND MONOPOLY REVENUE, 1940–1955

(In thousand yen)

	Major Tax Revenue						
Year	*Income Tax*	*Corporation Tax*	*Liquor Tax*	*Customs Duties*	*Monopoly Revenue*	*Total*	*Percentage of Income and Corporation Taxes to Total Revenue*
1940	1,488,679	182,873	285,174	146,094	352,170	4,217,342	39.64
1941	1,401,363	534,907	359,340	88,418	414,930	4,930,526	39.28
1942	2,236,191	775,946	433,791	56,665	568,440	7,528,897	40.01
1943	2,604,097	993,616	720,177	45,034	1,116,585	9,960,067	36.12
1944	4,040,581	1,326,514	833,943	15,633	1,197,682	12,862,828	41.73
1945	3,820,426	1,180,834	1,130,654	7,757	1,056,193	11,555,533	43.28
1946	12,240,677	1,316,262	2,378,118	15,199	7,325,970	55,553,414	24.40
1947	79,272,735	7,169,638	27,499,201	86,300	42,139,145	207,888,161	41.58
1948	190,831,800	27,900,319	54,793,616	260,520	101,914,238	455,560,359	48.01
1949	278,856,563	61,264,366	83,329,146	900,849	118,232,368	638,875,143	53.24
1950	220,134,192	83,790,196	105,375,665	1,625,620	114,456,978	571,721,544	54.09
1951	225,671,566	183,881,287	122,830,400	12,590,537	119,112,152	724,318,180	56.54
1952	269,918,668	186,008,406	139,290,492	21,427,097	134,575,871	843,030,995	54.08
1953	292,294,214	198,881,723	140,251,710	30,495,161	159,702,913	942,520,701	52.11
1954	285,632,260	200,251,940	151,213,045	24,641,140	125,654,083	934,083,497	52.02
1955	278,440,000	195,757,000	159,863,000	24,740,000	112,508,610	929,818,610	50.99

Note: During the above period, the income tax was separated from the corporation tax and the land tax was transferred from the national revenue to the local revenue. Hence Table 25 differs in style from Table 24.

mania; 1896, Austria; 1900, Spain; 1909, Hungary; 1914, France and Czechoslovakia; 1916, Russia; 1919, Greece, Luxemburg, and Belgium; 1920, Germany, Bulgaria, and Poland; 1922, Brazil and Rumania.

Several remarks are to be made concerning this list. In the first place, as to the adoption of the income tax by Great Britain, some believe that its origin is traceable to the triple assessment of 1798, while others contend it stems from the new income tax act of 1799. I have followed the former view. Popitz traces the origin of the national income tax in the United States to the first income tax act of July, 1862. In my view, however, the full-fledged income tax has its origin in the new income tax act of 1913, which took effect after the amendment of the federal Constitution.

Our Japanese income tax, adopted in 1887, is seventh in the order of adoption.

As in the case of all social systems, the time of the adoption and the content of the national income tax by different countries was naturally affected by various circumstances. This will be seen in the case of such countries as the United States, Germany, France and Great Britain.

Let us first take up the case of the United States. The state income tax had existed since the formation of the United States through the amalgamation of the different states, but it was in July, 1862, that the first federal income tax came into existence. It had only a feeble existence, so feeble in fact that it was soon abolished. It was readopted, but declared unconstitutional. Finally, an amendment was effected in the federal Constitution, thereby putting an end to the long dispute that "the federal income tax was a violation of the Constitution." The new income tax act was adopted in October, 1913, and has remained in force since that time.

In Germany, a tendency toward localism was strong because of the historical background of taxation and the iron law that "direct taxes belong to the separate states and indirect taxes to the empire." But after the adoption of the system of centralized government based upon the Weimar Constitution, the M. Erzberger reform was effected and the income tax was transferred from the state to the empire.

In France, the real taxes based on external standards has long held sway, and the income tax was regarded as opposed to the declaration of human rights which was the spirit of the French Revolution. Thus, more than two hundred bills for the adoption of the income tax were killed by the French legislature. It was as late as 1914, the year in which World War I broke out, that France adopted the income tax.

TABLE 26

IMPORTANT REVISION OF INCOME TAX, 1887, 1899, 1913,

	1887	*1899*	*1913*
Exemption limit	300 yen	CLASS III 300 yen	CLASS III 400 yen
Basic exemption	....	....	....
Earned income credit	....	....	CLASS III 10%
Exemption for each dependent	....	....	....
Exemption for physically handicapped person	....	....	....
Deduction for aged person, widow, working student	....	....	....
Deduction for miscellaneous loss	....	....	....
Deduction for medical care	....	....	....
Deduction for life insurance	....	....	....
Tax rate	Income over: 300 yen 1.0% 1,000 yen 1.5% 10,000 yen 2.0% 20,000 yen 2.5% 30,000 yen 3.0%	CLASS I INCOME 2.5% CLASS II INCOME 2.0% CLASS III INCOME over: 300 yen 1.0% 500 yen 1.2% 1,000 yen 1.5% 2,000 yen 1.7% 3,000 yen 2.0% 5,000 yen 2.5% 10,000 yen 3.0% 15,000 yen 3.5% 20,000 yen 4.0% 30,000 yen 4.5% 50,000 yen 5.0% 100,000 yen 5.5%	CLASS I INCOME *Category A* under: 5,000 yen 4.0% over: 5,000 yen 5.0% 10,000 yen 6.0% 15,000 yen 7.0% 20,000 yen 8.0% 30,000 yen 9.0% 50,000 yen 10.0% 70,000 yen 11.0% 100,000 yen 12.0% 200,000 yen 13.0% *Category B* 6.25% CLASS II INCOME Interest on local bonds 2.0% Interest on debentures 2.0% CLASS III INCOME under: 1,000 yen 2.5% over: 1,000 yen 3.5% 2,000 yen 4.5% 3,000 yen 5.5% 5,000 yen 7.0% 7,000 yen 8.5% 10,000 yen 10.0% 15,000 yen 12.0% 20,000 yen 14.0% 30,000 yen 16.0% 50,000 yen 18.0% 70,000 yen 20.0% 100,000 yen 22.0%
Special credit against income tax on dividend	....	....	....

1920, 1940, 1947, 1950, 1952, 1953, 1954, AND 1955

1920	*1940*	*1947*
CLASS III 800 yen	CLASSIFIED INCOME TAX Real estate 250 yen Dividends and interest 100 yen AGGREGATE INCOME TAX 5,000 yen	....
....	CLASSIFIED INCOME TAX Labor services 720 yen Enterprises 500 yen Forestry 500 yen	4,800 yen
CLASS III INCOME under: 12,000 yen 10.0% 6,000 yen 20.0%	AGGREGATE INCOME TAX under: 10,000 yen 10.0%	25% of earned income or 12,500 yen, whichever is smaller
CLASS III INCOME under: 1,000 yen 100 yen 2,000 yen 70 yen 3,000 yen 50 yen	CLASSIFIED INCOME TAX 12 yen	480 yen
....	....	....
....	....	....
....	....	....
....	....	....
....	6.0% of premium or 12 yen, whichever is smaller	....
CLASS I INCOME Excess 4.0%, 10.0%, 20.0% Reserve 5.0%, 10.0%, 20.0% Dividend 5.0% Liquidation 7.5% Foreign corporations 7.5% CLASS II INCOME Interest on local bonds 4.0% Interest on debentures and bank deposits for fixed periods 5.0% CLASS III INCOME under: 800 yen 0.5% over: 800 yen 1.0% 1,000 yen 2.0% 1,500 yen 3.0% 2,000 yen 4.0% 3,000 yen 5.0% 5,000 yen 6.5% 7,000 yen 8.0% 10,000 yen 9.5% 15,000 yen 11.0% 20,000 yen 13.0% 30,000 yen 15.0% 50,000 yen 17.0% 70,000 yen 19.0% 100,000 yen 21.0% 200,000 yen 23.0% 500,000 yen 25.0% 1,000,000 yen 27.0% 2,000,000 yen 30.0% 3,000,000 yen 33.0% 4,000,000 yen 36.0%	CLASSIFIED INCOME TAX Real estate 10.0% Bonds National 4.0% Local 9.0% Others 10.0% Enterprises Group A 8.5% Group B 7.5% Labor services 6.0% Forestry under: 1,600 yen 5.0% over: 1,600 yen 7.5% Retirement allowances under: 20,000 yen 6.0% over: 20,000 yen 12.0% 200,000 yen 25.0% 500,000 yen 40.0% AGGREGATE INCOME TAX over: 5,000 yen 10.0% 8,000 yen 15.0% 12,000 yen 20.0% 20.000 yen 25.0% 30,000 yen 30.0% 50,000 yen 35.0% 80,000 yen 40.0% 120,000 yen 45.0% 200,000 yen 50.0% 300,000 yen 55.0% 500,000 yen 60.0% 800,000 yen 65.0%	Income under: 10,000 yen 20% over: 10,000 yen 25% 15,000 yen 30% 20,000 yen 35% 30,000 yen 40% 40,000 yen 45% 50,000 yen 50% 70,000 yen 57% 90,000 yen 60% 120,000 yen 68% 150,000 yen 72% 200,000 yen 76% 250,000 yen 80% 300,000 yen 82% 500,000 yen 84% 1,000,000 yen 85%
....	....	....

TABLE 26 (Continued)

	1950	*1952*
Exemption limit	....	....
Basic exemption	25,000 yen	50,000 yen
Earned income credit	15% of earned income or 30,000 yen, whichever is smaller	15% of earned income or 30,000 yen, whichever is smaller
Exemption for each dependent	12,000 yen	First three dependents 20,000 yen Others 15,000 yen
Exemption for physically handicapped person	12,000 yen	4,000 yen
Deduction for aged person, widow, working student	....	4,000 yen
Deduction for miscellaneous loss	Income Tax Law, Article 11 (3)	Article 11 (3)
Deduction for medical care	Article 11 (4)	Article 11 (4)
Deduction for life insurance	....	Amount of premium or 4,000 yen, whichever is smaller
Tax rate	Income under: 50,000 yen 20% over: 50,000 yen 25% 80,000 yen 30% 100,000 yen 35% 120,000 yen 40% 150,000 yen 45% 200,000 yen 50% 500,000 yen 55%	Income under: 80,000 yen 20% over: 80,000 yen 25% 120,000 yen 30% 200,000 yen 35% 300,000 yen 40% 500,000 yen 45% 1,000,000 yen 50% 2,000,000 yen 55%
Special credit against income tax on dividend	25% of dividend income	25% of dividend income

TABLE 26 (Continued)

1953	*1954*	*1955*
....	....	....
60,000 yen	70,000 yen	80,000 yen
15% of earned income or 45,000 yen, whichever is smaller	15% of earned income or 45,000 yen, whichever is smaller	15% of earned income or 60,000 yen, whichever is smaller
First dependent 35,000 yen Second and third 20,000 yen Others 15,000 yen	First dependent 40,000 yen Second and third 25,000 yen Others 15,000 yen	First dependent 40,000 yen Second and third 25,000 yen Others 15,000 yen
4,000 yen	4,000 yen	5,000 yen
4,000 yen	4,000 yen	5,000 yen
Article 11 (3)	Article 11 (3)	Article 11 (3)
Article 11 (4)	Article 11 (4)	Article 11 (4)
Amount of premium or 8,000 yen, whichever is smaller	Amount of premium or 12,000 yen, whichever is smaller	Amount of premium or 15,000 yen, whichever is smaller
Income under: 20,000 yen 15% over: 20,000 yen 20% 70,000 yen 25% 120,000 yen 30% 200,000 yen 35% 300,000 yen 40% 500,000 yen 45% 1,000,000 yen 50% 2,000,000 yen 55% 3,000,000 yen 60% 5,000,000 yen 65%	Income under: 20,000 yen 15% over: 20,000 yen 20% 70,000 yen 25% 120,000 yen 30% 200,000 yen 35% 300,000 yen 40% 500,000 yen 45% 1,000,000 yen 50% 2,000,000 yen 55% 3,000,000 yen 60% 5,000,000 yen 65%	Income under: 30,000 yen 15% over: 30,000 yen 20% 80,000 yen 25% 150,000 yen 30% 300,000 yen 35% 500,000 yen 40% 800,000 yen 45% 1,200,000 yen 50% 2,000,000 yen 55% 3,000,000 yen 60% 5,000,000 yen 65%
25% of dividend income	25% of dividend income	30% of dividend income

TABLE 27

	1940		1947	
TAX RATE FOR NORMAL INCOME				
Domestic		18%		35%
Special		6%		25%
Foreign		28%		45%
TAX RATE FOR EXCESS INCOME	*Extraordinary profit tax*		*Excess profit tax*	
	Excess of normal income over 10% of the amount of capital employed:		Excess of normal income over 10% of the amount of capital employed	10%
	under average profit of 1934–36	25%	Excess of normal income over 20% of the amount of capital employed	20%
	over average profit of 1934–36 but under 30% of the amount of capital employed	45%	Excess of normal income over 30% of the amount of capital employed	30%
	over 30% of the amount of capital employed	65%		
TAX RATE FOR INCOME AT LIQUIDATION				
Reserves				20%
Other accounts		18%		45%
TAX RATE FOR CAPITAL EMPLOYED		0.15%		0.5%
TAX RATE FOR FAMILY CORPORATION				
Additional tax on excess reserves	*Excess reserve tax*		*Excess reserve tax*	
	Income		Income	
	under: 50,000 yen	20%	under: 100,000 yen	35%
	over: 50,000 yen	30%	over: 100,000 yen	60%
	100,000 yen	40%	200,000 yen	70%
	500,000 yen	50%	500,000 yen	75%
	1,000,000 yen	65%	1,000,000 yen	80%
Reserves				

IMPORTANT REVISIONS OF CORPORATION TAX, 1940, 1947, 1952, 1953, 1954, AND 1955

1952	*1953*	*1954*	*1955*
42%	42%	42%	under 500,000 yen 35% over 500,000 yen 40%
35%	35%	35%	30%
42%	42%	42%	under 500,000 yen 35% over 500,000 yen 40%
	20%	20%	20%
	Normal corporation 46% Special corporation 41%	Normal corporation 46% Special corporation 41%	Normal corporation 45% Special corporation 40%
Reserve for each accounting period over 500,000 yen 5%	Reserve for each accounting period over 1,000,000 yen, or 25% of capital, whichever is higher 5%	Newly accumulated part of reserve for each accounting period over 1,000,000 yen, or 25% of capital, whichever is higher 10%	10% over 1,000,000 yen, or 25% of capital, whichever is higher

In the case of Great Britain, an income tax law was enacted in 1798 only to be abolished in 1802. It was readopted in 1803, repealed in 1816. After being readopted in 1842, it remained as a permanent tax in the British system. The income tax of 1803 was a schedule based on the principle of withholding at source, incomes being classified as A, B, C, D, and E. In 1910 Mr. Lloyd George adopted a supertax on income which was later renamed as the surtax. This played the role of an aggregate income tax, and it and the established schedule system constituted the British income tax.

Professor E.R.A. Seligman (E.R.A. Seligman, "Income Tax," *Encyclopedia of the Social Sciences,* VII, 626) says that the origin of the income tax is closely associated with the development of commerce and industry, with the widespread diffusion of the money economy and the consequent emergence of new forms of wealth that could not be reached by older forms of taxation. These factors do not, to my mind, constitute a sufficient cause. In order to establish an income tax in a country the national political and social conditions must be satisfied. We have seen that the constitutional provisions of the United States retarded the development of the income tax, the German political principle which demanded apportionment of financial resources among states delayed the adoption of a national income tax, and the spirit of liberty of the French Revolution prevented the passage of an income tax law until the outbreak of World War I. Again, even England, where the industrial revolution was experienced earlier than in other countries, had to be content with the classified income tax until 1910, having been hampered by its own tradition. These facts show that the whole taxation system of a country, as in the case of the income tax above cited, is greatly influenced by special national circumstances.

The Japanese income tax law was first established in 1887. Although in the sense of the present science of finance the law of 1887 was a very simple one, it did provide progressive taxation on the principle of aggregate income taxation, and as such, it was more advanced than the system of England or Italy at the time. Revisions were made in 1899, 1920, 1940, and a revolutionary revision in 1950. As many as forty minor revisions can be counted. In other countries the income tax was still in its infancy in the 1880s, without exception. For instance, the British income tax at that time was no more than proportional tax on the withholding-at-source basis, although it had assumed a permanent nature by then, outlasting the periods of wartime taxation and temporary taxation. In the United States, the federal income tax was abolished in 1871 and revived in 1894. France was busily engaged in the readjustment following the Franco-Prussian War and in no mood to consider an income tax. In Italy, the tax had existed as early as 1864 and a large-scale revision was made in 1877 which laid the foundation of the present system, but in those days it was but a crude form (*imposta sui redditi della ricchezza mobile*).

It is a surprising fact that a country like Japan, which was late in entering into the world theater, had an income tax law of modern color, ahead of other advanced countries. The explanation is that the finance of Japan was virgin soil in which any new system could grow. At the recommendation of foreign financial advisers, pioneers boldly adopted the income tax system, a system considered most advanced at that time.

In European countries as in America it would have been difficult to adopt a new system without first destroying a well-rooted one. In Japan there was no strong system to uproot. On the other hand, the very fact that a modern system was planted in uncultivated land was responsible for the weakness of the system itself, that is the law went ahead and enforcement lagged behind. It was "an income tax law with no fruit of income."

PART FOUR

Some Special Research

VIII. *The Effect of Taxation on the Disparity between Rich and Poor*

WHILE there are several social principles in taxation, the most important fact that exists in society and needs adjustment is the disparity between rich and poor. An attempt has been made to narrow this disparity either by levying progressive taxes or by some other means.

There are three different methods of measuring the disparity between rich and poor. In the "comparison method" the first step is to ascertain the ratio between the total number of persons with income and the number of those with income above or below a certain amount; the second step is to find the ratio between the total amount of incomes and the amount above or below a certain amount; these two ratios are then compared. The larger the difference between them, the more uneven is the distribution of incomes. What may be termed the "simple method" is based on a frequency distribution of incomes. The third method is to measure the degree of dispersion of incomes by a single index which can be calculated from the degree of dispersion shown in the frequency distribution of incomes. This method requires a complicated calculation but it excels other methods, as the disparity can be more accurately shown by a single dispersion degree of incomes. Most contemporary statisticians base their study on this method. Among the more than ten applications of this principle, "Pareto's Equation" is the most popular and widely known.

Colin Clark (*The Conditions of Economic Progress,* 1939, p. 425) adopted α of Pareto's Equation when he attempted to make an international comparison of the distribution of national incomes during the period from 1812 to 1936. Using his figures from 1914 to 1936 and adding to them the missing portion pertaining to Japan, an international comparison of the distribution of the national incomes since World War I is shown in the Table 28.

While α of Pareto's Equation shows the inequality of income distribution in inverse proportion, the coefficient of mean difference (relative

TABLE 28

INTERNATIONAL COMPARISON OF α OF PARETO'S EQUATION, 1914–1936

Year	*England*	*United States*	*Germany*	*France*	*Japan*	*Russia*	*Denmark*	*Australia*	*New Zealand*	*Holland*	*Hungary*	*Finland*
1914	...	1.54	1.56	...	1.89	...	...	...	...	...	...	...
1915	...	1.40	...	...	1.89	...	...	...	...	...	...	...
1916	...	1.34	...	...	1.78	...	...	...	...	...	...	...
1917	...	1.49	...	...	1.58	...	...	...	...	...	...	...
1918	...	1.65	...	...	1.55	...	...	...	...	...	...	...
1919	...	1.71	...	...	1.61	...	...	...	...	...	...	...
1920	...	1.82	...	...	1.85	...	...	...	...	...	...	...
1921	...	1.90	...	...	1.74	...	...	...	...	...	...	...
1922	...	1.71	...	...	1.75	...	...	...	...	...	...	...
1923	...	1.73	...	...	1.72	2.07	...	...	...	...	...	...
1924	...	1.67	...	...	1.76	1.96	...	...	...	...	...	...
1925	...	1.54	...	...	1.71	...	...	...	...	...	...	...
1926	...	1.55	1.79	...	1.72	...	...	...	...	...	...	...
1927	...	1.52	...	...	1.68	...	...	...	...	...	...	...
1928	...	1.42	1.78	...	1.67	...	...	...	...	...	...	...
1929	1.61	1.42	...	...	1.66	...	...	...	...	...	...	...
1930	...	1.62	...	...	1.66	...	...	...	...	...	...	...
1931	...	1.71	...	1.75	1.70	...	...	...	...	1.70	...	...
1932	1.68	1.76	1.77	...	1.59	...	...	...	...	...	1.64	...
1933	...	1.70	...	...	1.60	...	...	...	...	...	...	...
1934	...	1.77	1.96	1.82	1.65	...	...	2.25	2.21	...	...	2.03
1935	...	1.75	...	...	1.68	...	1.94	...	...	...	...	...
1936	...	1.72	...	...	1.66	...	...	...	...	...	...	...

mean difference) shows the inequality of income distribution in direct proportion. Here is Simpson's method, one of the ways of computing coefficient of mean difference (L. von Bortkiewicz's "Die Disparitatsmasse der Einkommenstatistik," *Bulletin de L'Institut International de Statistique,* Tokio, 1930):

Let N be the number of income earners, and S the sum total of the incomes of all earners. Then make a frequency distribution according to the income:

Let x_1 be the number of income earners who get less than $\frac{S}{4}$, e.g., Q_1 of the total income.

Let x_2 be the number of income earners who get less than $\frac{S}{2}$, e.g., Q_2 of the total income.

Let x_3 be the number of income earners who get less than $\frac{3}{4}$S, e.g., Q_3 of the total income.

$$\text{Also } \frac{x_1}{N} = y_1, \quad \frac{x_2}{N} = y_2, \quad \frac{x_3}{N} = y_3.$$

Then we have the following equation.

$$N = \frac{2\{2(y_1 + y_3) + y_2 - 2.5\}}{3}$$

The following result was obtained by computing the coefficient of mean difference from 1887 up to 1952, using the same data of income tax statistics in Japan as was used for the computation of α of Pareto's equation.

Table 29 shows α of Pareto's equation and η of Simpson's method to illustrate the inequality of income distribution, the former in inverse proportion and the latter in direct proportion.

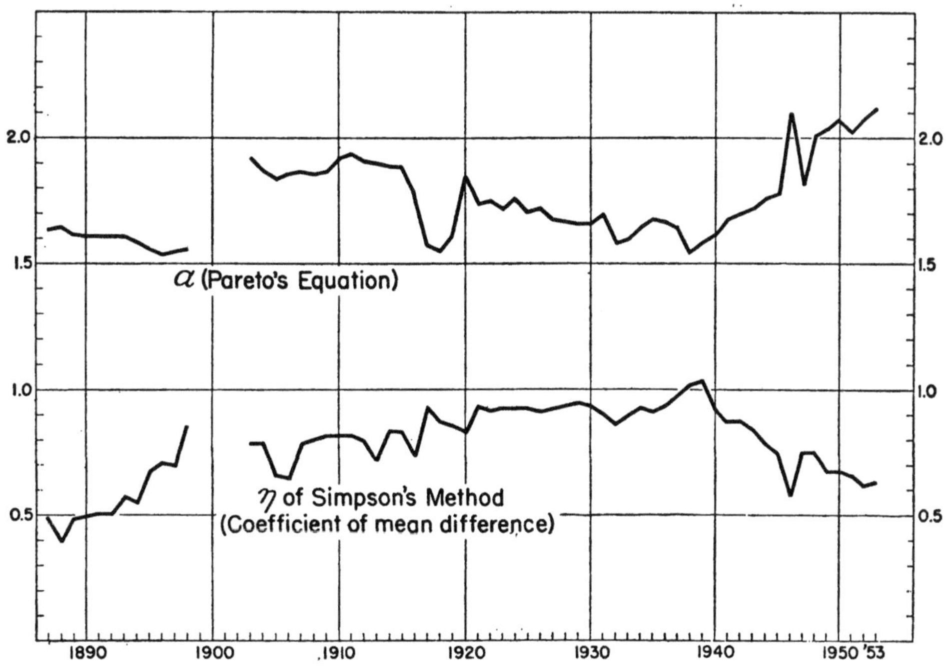

CHART 4

INDEX OF DISPARITY BETWEEN RICH AND POOR IN JAPAN, 1887–1953

TABLE 29

A COMPARISON OF α OF PARETO'S EQUATION AND η OF SIMPSON'S METHOD, 1887–1952

Year	α (*Pareto's Equation*)	η *of Simpson's Method* (*Coefficient of mean difference*)
1887	1.6378	0.4869
1888	1.6507	0.3973
1889	1.6159	0.4947
1890	1.6109	0.5014
1891	1.6145	0.5148
1892	1.6099	0.5142
1893	1.6113	0.5730
1894	1.5911	0.5502
1895	1.5626	0.6826
1896	1.5413	0.7076
1897	1.5454	0.7033
1898	1.5604	0.8573
1899	.....	.....
1900	.....	.....
1901	.....	.....
1902	.....	.....
1903	1.9177	0.7863
1904	1.8744	0.7934
1905	1.8442	0.6554
1906	1.8634	0.6546
1907	1.8670	0.7940
1908	1.8589	0.7964
1909	1.8722	0.8246
1910	1.9233	0.8238
1911	1.9385	0.8215
1912	1.9132	0.7979
1913	1.9026	0.7226
1914	1.8890	0.8349
1915	1.8908	0.8369
1916	1.7773	0.7352
1917	1.5785	0.9278
1918	1.5472	0.8821
1919	1.6117	0.8583
1920	1.8481	0.8357
1921	1.7388	0.9359
1922	1.7495	0.9176
1923	1.7230	0.9294
1924	1.7585	0.9253
1925	1.7141	0.9206
1926	1.7236	0.9156
1927	1.6813	0.9317
1928	1.6700	0.9362
1929	1.6649	0.9488
1930	1.6619	0.9360
1931	1.7006	0.9073

TABLE 29 (Continued)

Year	α (*Pareto's Equation*)	η of *Simpson's Method* (*Coefficient of mean difference*)
1932	1.5904	0.8739
1933	1.6030	0.9034
1934	1.6484	0.9306
1935	1.6758	0.9208
1936	1.6644	0.9391
1937	1.6511	0.9829
1938	1.5465	1.0169
1939	1.5937	1.0435
1940	1.6168	0.9230
1941	1.6783	0.8808
1942	1.6986	0.8778
1943	1.7208	0.8544
1944	1.7602	0.7939
1945	1.7777	0.7466
1946	2.1030	0.5775
1947	1.8204	0.7541
1948	2.0092	0.7453
1949	2.0340	0.6773
1950	2.0818	0.6783
1951	1.9322	0.6555
1952	1.9762	0.6246

THE DIFFERENCE IN THE EFFECT ON THE DISPARITY BETWEEN RICH AND POOR OF WORLD WARS I AND II

War brings out a striking change in the distribution of incomes. It has sometimes been questioned whether war is economically profitable. Japan found World War I profitable because she kept out of the major part of the struggle throughout. But World War II was an entirely different matter. It was common sense to think that the war was a lost cause for Japan from the beginning. Let us compare the effect of the two wars on distribution of income between rich and poor.

At the time of World War I, our income tax was grouped into Classes I, II, and III. Class III income, levied on the principle of progressive rates, was a convenient yardstick for our purpose. Taking 1914 as a prewar year and 1918 as a postwar year, Table 30 was prepared to illustrate the distribution of incomes of these two years.

Both the number of taxpaying families and the amount of incomes show that the increase of large incomes from 1914 to 1918 far exceeds that of middle and small incomes, thus showing that the disparity between rich and poor became very prominent.

Let us now turn to World War II. The revision of 1941 provided for two classes of taxes, classified income tax and aggregate income tax. As the aggregate tax operated on the progressive basis as a rule, the distribution of incomes by each class of large and small incomes could be traced from the data of the aggregate income tax. Taking the year 1941 as prewar and 1945 as postwar year, the result of the study of the number of taxpaying families and the amount of incomes of these two years is summarized in Table 31.

As shown in Table 31, the result of the prewar and postwar periods of the World War II is exactly the opposite of World War I. The increase is seen only in middle and small incomes in the number of taxpaying families as well as the amount of incomes, while large incomes are rather contracted, indicating that the disparity between rich and poor was lessened.

The foregoing is the result obtained by using unadjusted figures in order to show the disparity between rich and poor, reckoned by the actual number of taxpaying families and the actual amount of incomes.

TABLE 30

DISTRIBUTION OF INCOMES BEFORE AND AFTER WORLD WAR I

Income Class (In yen)	Number of Taxpaying Families		Amount of Incomes (In thousand yen)		Percentage of 1918 (1914 = 100)	
	1914	*1918*	*1914*	*1918*	*Taxpaying Families*	Income
400– 500	229,056	}				
500– 700	205,252	340,467 }	266,452 }	} 281,078	165	
700– 1,000	127,290	186,094 }			146	
1,000– 2,000	110,051	159,745	149,895	218,265	145	146
2,000– 3,000	26,883	42,026	65,132	102,073	156	157
3,000– 5,000	16,897	27,584	63,929	105,064	163	164
5,000– 7,000	5,289	9,740	30,947	57,046	184	184
7,000– 10,000	3,104	6,031	25,658	50,049	194	195
10,000– 15,000	1,809	3,687	21,817	44,546	204	204
15,000– 20,000	687	1,574	11,826	27,141	229	230
20,000– 30,000	467	1,191	11,147	28,674	255	257
30,000– 50,000	206	731	7,643	27,736	355	363
50,000– 70,000	57	232	3,252	13,510	407	415
70,000–100,000	26	164	2,174	13,548	631	623
Over 100,000	15	214	2,711	49,335	1,427	1,820
Total	727,089	799,480	662,589	1,018,070		
(Over 500)	(498,033)[a]		(396,137)[b]	(736,992)[c]	(157)	(186)

[a] 498,033 = 727,089 – 229,056.
[b] 396,137 = 662,589 – 266,452.
[c] 736,992 = 1,018,070 – 281,078.

TABLE 31

DISTRIBUTION OF INCOME IMMEDIATELY BEFORE AND AFTER WORLD WAR II

Income Class (In yen)	Number of Taxpaying Families		Amount of Incomes (In thousand yen)		Percentage of 1945 (1941 = 100)	
	1941	*1945*	*1941*	*1945*	*Tax-paying Families*	*Income*
3,000– 5,000		674,534		2,595,416		
5,000– 8,000	125,650	237,044	792,093	1,484,370	189	187
8,000– 12,000	66,179	110,017	642,711	1,068,788	166	166
12,000– 20,000	41,260	54,525	624,795	820,382	132	131
20,000– 30,000	15,496	19,128	374,779	464,764	123	124
30,000– 50,000	9,882	11,509	374,851	436,146	116	116
50,000– 80,000	4,107	4,469	254,258	275,158	109	108
80,000–120,000	1,679	1,798	161,308	169,627	107	105
120,000–200,000	1,060	927	159,383	139,738	87	72
200,000–300,000	375	345	90,529	84,740	92	94
300,000–500,000	208	209	78,682	81,513	100	104
Over 500,000	123	111	139,335	117,524	90	84
Total	266,019	1,114,616	3,692,729	7,738,170		
(Over 5,000)		(440,082) [a]		(5,142,754) [b]	(165)	(139)

[a] 440,082 = 1,114,616 – 674,534.
[b] 5,142,754 = 7,738,170 – 2,595,416.

The unadjusted figures have the advantage of realism but because they contain certain unavoidable irregularities they lack the accuracy and simplicity for finding a tendency. It may well be worthwhile to seek a single index of the disparity by adjusting the number of taxpaying families and the amount of incomes.

The movement of the index in Chart 5 points to the conclusion derived from Tables 30 and 31. So also α of Pareto's Equation, which indicates that the index number 1.8890 in 1914 shrank to 1.5472 in 1918, showing the disparity between rich and poor widened during World War I, whereas the index number 1.6783 in 1941 climbed up to 1.7777 in 1945, showing the disparity narrowed during World War II. Particular attention should be called to the fact that, despite so large a difference as 0.3418 between the prewar and postwar periods of World War I, the difference between the corresponding periods of World War II is only 0.0994, offering conclusive evidence that the degree of change during World War II is much smaller than that during World War I. Also the movement of η (coefficient of mean difference) confirms the fact. η indicates that the coefficient 0.8349 in1914 climbed to 0.8821 in 1918, demonstrating that the inequality of income distribution ex-

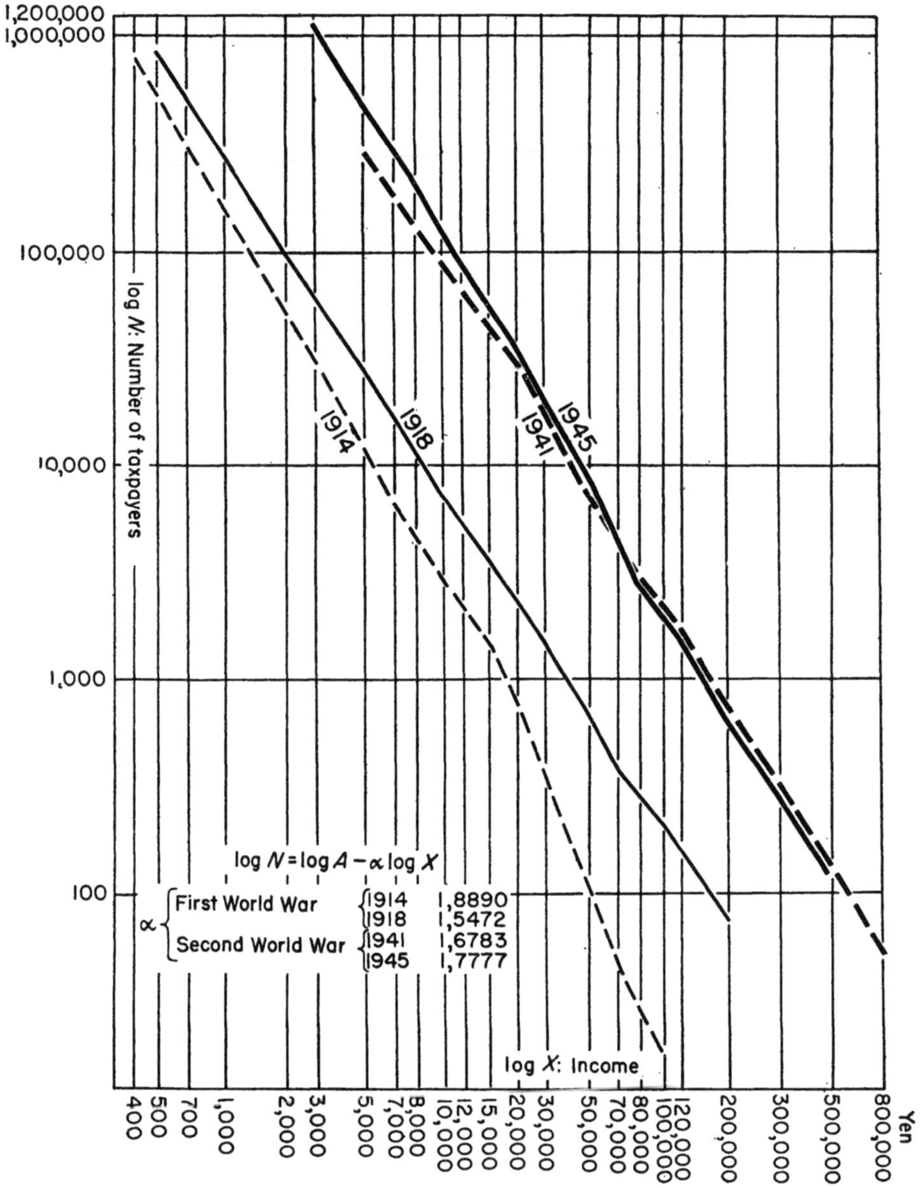

CHART 5

COMPARISON OF α OF PARETO'S EQUATION DURING WORLD WAR I AND WORLD WAR II

panded during World War I, whereas the coefficient 0.9230 in 1940 shrank to 0.7466 in 1945, demonstrating that the inequality narrowed during World War II. The fact that wars smoothed the sharp edge of disparity between rich and poor was pointed out in figures presented by Professor Bowley (*Some Economic Consequences of the Great War*, 1930, p. 131) in England at the time of World War I. In Japan, the same thing happened during World War II while quite the opposite phenomenon appeared during World War I.

THE EFFECT OF TAXATION ON THE DISTRIBUTION OF NATIONAL INCOME

The fact that the disparity between rich and poor was softened in Japan before and after World War II has so far been proved inductively. It can be proved deductively as well. In a prolonged warfare, particularly a lost war which has assumed the aspect of total war, there is bound to appear a strong trend toward tendency of equalization of income. What accelerates the disparity between rich and poor usually consists of incomes from enterprises and assets, because the limits of earned incomes do not permit a vast difference between maximum and minimum. Moreover, during the war period, the land income and house income were controlled by the Land, House, Rent Control Ordinance, and liquid incomes were also restricted by the Dividends Restriction Ordinance. Even earned incomes suffered a similar restriction under wage controls. As to enterprise incomes of corporations and individuals, the bulk was taken away by the national or local government under the extraordinary profit tax and other taxes. These procedures, no doubt, narrowed the disparity between rich and poor. In short, in order to carry out total war, the free economic activity of individuals was kept under strict control, resulting in equalization of income distribution.

These control measures were not lifted for some time after the war. Furthermore, the devaluation of currency due to inflation and the imposition of the war indemnity special tax and the capital levy seriously curtailed the income from properties and, in some cases, even made inroads upon capital, reducing the propertied classes of the old days to the declining classes. A striking change also took place in earned incomes. Payment was no longer on the basis of ability but on a minimum living cost. Witness the absurd instance of a watchman in a municipal office with a large family who received higher pay than an assistant mayor with a small family.

The effect of taxation on the disparity between rich and poor can be seen in two ways. The one is ordinary taxes which are collected regularly every year and the other is temporary taxes such as the extraordinary profit tax, the capital levy, and the war indemnity tax.

The national finance is closely interrelated with private economy and its effect on the distribution of income is also twofold. The one is government disbursements, bond issues and their retirement, etc., and the other is the collection of taxes. There is no question that both affect the distribution of income but, whereas the effect of the former is in a more or less roundabout way, that of the latter is direct. Direct taxes, in case of withholding income tax, are levied simultaneously with the distribution of incomes and in case of the self-assessment income tax, a portion of incomes is likewise taken away after distribution. On the other hand, indirect taxes are automatically collected from every individual who consumes articles in which price taxes are included. As Professor Bowley pointed out and as Colin Clark remarked in a chapter "Redistribution of Incomes through Taxation" in his *National Income and Outlay* (1937), one of the latest striking characteristics of the distribution of incomes is high progressive rates for large incomes, and the bulk of incomes thus collected is redistributed through the vertical processes in the form of old-age pensions, unemployment allowances, and

TABLE 32

COMPARISON OF INCOME DISTRIBUTION BY PERCENT BEFORE AND AFTER PAYMENT OF THE AGGREGATE INCOME TAX

Income Class	*Amount of Incomes before Taxation*		*Tax Rate*		*Amount of Incomes after Taxation*	
(In yen)	*1941*	*1945*	*1941*	*1945*	*1941*	*1945*
5,000– 8,000	21.5	28.9	2.0	5.6	24.6	33.3
8,000– 12,000	17.4	20.8	5.7	10.1	19.1	22.8
12,000– 20,000	16.9	16.0	9.9	15.6	17.9	16.4
20,000– 30,000	10.1	9.0	14.3	21.7	10.2	8.6
30,000– 50,000	10.2	8.5	18.9	27.7	9.7	7.5
50,000– 80,000	6.9	5.3	23.8	33.7	6.1	4.3
80,000–120,000	4.4	3.3	28.3	39.4	3.7	2.4
120,000–200,000	4.3	2.7	33.3	44.7	3.4	1.8
200,000–300,000	2.5	1.6	38.3	49.9	1.8	1.0
300,000–500,000	2.1	1.6	43.6	54.8	1.4	0.9
Over 500,000	3.7	2.3	54.2	65.7	2.0	1.0
Total	100.0	100.0	14.7	18.0	100.0	100.0

TABLE 33

DISTRIBUTION OF INCOME DURING AND AFTER WORLD WAR II

Income Class (In yen)	1942 Number of Taxpaying Families	1942 Amount of Incomes (In thousand yen)	1943 Number of Taxpaying Families	1943 Amount of Incomes (In thousand yen)
3,000– 5,000	353,701	1,363,551	448,717	1,725,902
5,000– 8,000	179,895	1,129,900	217,628	1,361,394
8,000– 12,000	97,217	944,065	109,449	1,066,939
12,000– 20,000	55,303	832,886	60,194	905,957
20,000– 30,000	19,792	478,525	20,950	505,931
30,000– 50,000	11,818	447,398	12,567	475,325
50,000– 80,000	4,828	298,174	5,083	313,672
80,000–120,000	1,881	180,613	2,048	197,733
120,000–200,000	1,108	167,317	1,151	174,370
200,000–300,000	390	94,791	428	103,141
300,000–500,000	226	85,030	239	89,019
Over 500,000	125	134,836	134	143,919
Total	726,284	6,157,091	878,588	7,063,309

1942: $\log N = 11.8731054 - 1.6986 \log x$; $\frac{2\{2(Y_1 + y_3) + y_2 - 2.5\}}{3} = 0.87784$

1943: $\log N = 12.0117726 - 1.7208 \log x$; $\frac{2\{2(y_1 + y_3) + y_2 - 2.5\}}{3} = 0.85442$

Income Class (In thousand yen)	1948 Number of Taxpaying Families	1948 Amount of Incomes (In thousand yen)	1949 Number of Taxpaying Families	1949 Amount of Incomes (In thousand yen)
10.325– 15 } 15– 20 }	269,886	4,841,715		
15– 20			118,253	2,519,371
20– 40	1,148,042	39,260,417	552,110	21,113,171
40– 70	2,308,921	135,999,637	1,694,158	106,245,284
70– 100	1,677,664	144,928,872	1,816,450	166,021,516
100– 150	1,135,472	140,288,981	1,664,563	217,018,660
150– 200	421,402	74,679,249	805,575	143,877,405
200– 220	102,209	21,580,076 }	458,712 }	105,101,345 }
220– 250	104,051	24,815,731 }		
250– 300	91,931	25,732,841	217,049	60,247,539
300– 500	96,066	37,725,513	207,181	83,184,936
500– 700	23,967	14,534,441	45,932	27,577,729
700–1,000	12,175	10,167,479	20,080	16,696,381
1,000–2,000	6,345	8,679,335	7,911	10,664,145
2,000–5,000	1,462	4,194,370	1,689	4,819,650
Over 5,000	196	1,836,404	277	2,445,427
Total	7,399,787	689,265,060	7,609,940	967,532,659

1948: $\log N = 16.0054135 - 2.0092 \log x$; $\frac{2\{2(y_1 + y_3) + y_2 - 2.5\}}{3} = 0.7453$

1949: $\log N = 16.139998 - 2.0378 \log x$; $\frac{2\{2(y_1 + y_3) + y_2 - 2.5\}}{3} = 0.6603$

public works, transferring income from large-income earners to small-income pockets. In contrast to direct taxes, indirect taxes have a retrogressive effect. If the rate for the indirect tax is raised and its revenue is redistributed in the form of payment of interest on national bonds, the effect will be quite opposite to the case of direct tax, creating a tendency of wealth of multitude being absorbed by large-income earners. While both direct and indirect taxes have an important bearing on redistribution of national incomes, the progressive effect of direct tax is considered most important in all taxation systems of many countries in the world.

As the aggregate income tax is imposing progressive rates on incomes of each class, a study was made to find out how it affected the disparity between rich and poor. The result is shown in Table 32.

Taking 100 as a basic index number for the total amount of incomes before tax payment, Table 32 shows in percentages how those incomes were distributed among various classes. For the same incomes after taxation, an index number 100 was also used for the balance after the progressive tax had been levied to show how the balance was distributed. It is of course desirable to have the disparity between rich and poor leveled off, but if carried too far this kills productive incentive and interferes with industrial activities.

We have so far studied how the income tax, the main direct tax, affects the distribution of national income. Our findings can more or less be applied to other countries, although in some of them the direct tax also includes revenue taxes (such as the land tax, house tax, and business tax), while others look upon them as the revenue sources for local finance. It is therefore necessary to extend our study to national and local revenue taxes to obtain a complete view of the effect of direct tax on the distribution of national income.

Now, let us turn to indirect taxes. Indirect taxes, the backbone of which are the liquor tax and the tobacco tax, affect the distribution of national income in an opposite manner than does the aggregate income tax. Indirect taxes, in their nature, involve a more complicated process than do direct taxes. Therefore, for a study of their effect on the distribution of national income, we must resort to a family budgeting method, tabulating all miscellaneous expense items such as liquor, tobacco, movie tickets, and so on, but our study is bound to include many illogical hypotheses, and an accurate conclusion, such as was reached in the case of the income tax, cannot be obtained.

IX. *A Financial Survey of Sixty-seven Municipalities within a Radius of 16 Kilometers of the City of Osaka*

THE study advanced in Parts I, II, and III was principally devoted to national finance. This chapter deals with local finance primarily from the local point of view.

As stated in Chapter I, taking an average of the five years from 1932 to 1936 as a basis, commodity prices in 1952 advanced 365 times (Table I) against 300 times (Table 5) for national expenditure, indicating that the expansion of the national budget is smaller than the advance in commodity prices. As shown in Table 34, the increase of local finance, however, was 384 times greater—not only than the increase of national finance but also larger than the price advance. In the local field, the increase of prefectural finance was far the largest, 556 times; for towns and villages it was 360 times; and the least increase was seen in the city finance, 245 times. Table 34 also shows how national, prefectural, city, town and village expenditures have moved in relation to the advance of commodity prices in the period of 1940 to 1952.

There is one thing, however, to be reckoned with in making such a comparison. That is, while the figures for national finance are derived from a single source, those for local finance are the aggregate for 46 prefectures, 400 cities, and 8,362 towns and villages, as listed on June 1, 1954. When we cite the increase in local finance over the average of 1932-36, we are citing an average increase for all these local entities; if we examine them individually we find that some are far above average and others much below it. Accurate comparison is made more difficult by frequent changes in the status of local bodies, such as the formation of a new city by merging several towns or villages, or the expansion of a city area by amalgamating with it adjoining cities or towns. Since it is beyond the author's ability to analyze the finance of every local civic unit—there are 8,808 in all—a certain model area has been selected and a bird's-eye-view of finance is sketched for this.

TABLE 34

INDEX OF NATIONAL AND LOCAL EXPENDITURE

	Wholesale Price Index in Tokyo	National Expenditure (Net Total of General Account and Special Accounts)	Local Expenditure [a]			
			Prefectures	Cities	Towns and Villages	Total
1932–36 average	100	100	100	100	100	100
1940	171	285	162	102	102	123
1941	183	470	184	111	116	138
1942	200	588	194	124	129	150
1943	214	829	293	126	136	187
1944	242	1,604	263	109	124	167
1945	366	2,074	330	142	156	212
1946	1,701	3,226	2,134	505	807	1,149
1947	5,035	7,349	6,724	1,791	3,576	3,931
1948	13,378	17,878	17,412	5,822	10,860	11,028
1949	21,832	32,285	27,163	10,248	16,424	17,590
1950	25,811	33,425	34,781	15,841	24,053	24,342
1951	35,755	29,268	45,983	21,200	29,122	31,709
1952	36,536	29,993	56,636	24,524	36,067	38,420
1953	38,510	33,624				
1954		34,508				

[a] Local expenditure includes enterprise accounts.

LOCAL FINANCE IN A SOCIAL AND ECONOMIC REGION

The region of social and economic life does not necessarily coincide with the administrative division. Localities in the same administrative unit may differ from each other socially and economically and in these respects may more closely resemble another locality in a different administrative unit. An attempt is therefore made in this section to study local finance in a social and economic region rather than an administrative region. Using data prepared by the Financc Bureau of the city of Osaka and the Administrative Section of the Osaka Prefecture on the finance of neighboring towns and villages, the study extends over the last twenty years. The area covered by the survey is shown in the accompanying diagram, which includes twelve cities and fifty-five towns and villages within a radius of sixteen kilometers from the municipal building in Osaka. Sixteen kilometers is a distance easily covered in an hour by present transportation facilities and the people within this area are likely to have close similarities in social and economic life. All sixty-seven cities, towns, and villages belong to Osaka Prefecture with the exception of two cities, Amagasaki and Itami, which are administered by Hyogo Prefecture. As of 1950, the total area is 748,506 square kilometers; the population, 3,476,511 in 1950 (3,587,672 in

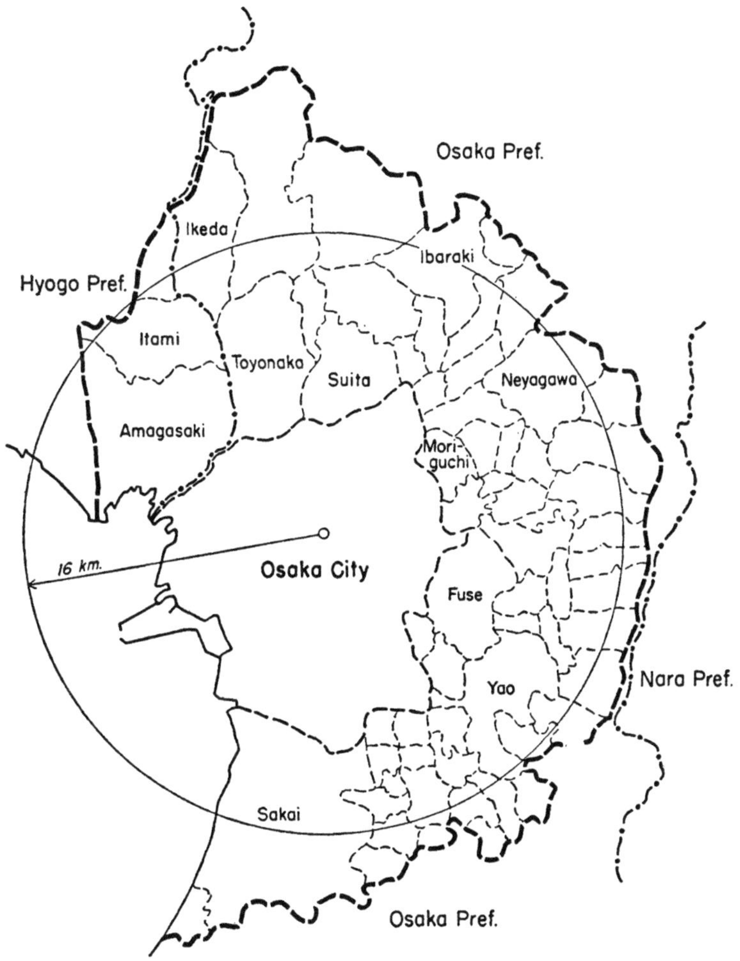

1953), has a density of 4,645 per square kilometer. The details are given in Table 35.

The areal proportion of cities and county districts in 1950 were 62.3 percent and 37.7 percent respectively and the population was 87.8 percent for the former and 12.2 percent for the latter. The population ratio became 89 percent and 11 percent, respectively, in 1953. The

TABLE 35

AREA AND POPULATION OF 67 MUNICIPALITIES

	Population					*Area (in sq. km.), 1950*	*Density of Population, 1950*
	1933	*1940*	*1945*	*1950*	*1953*		
Cities:							
Osaka	2,654,000	3,252,340	1,102,959	1,956,136	2,341,019	187,440	10,436
Amagasaki	57,653	270,879	133,051	279,264	339,116	49,200	5,676
Sakai	126,524	182,147	165,854	213,688	230,993	51,483	4,151
Fuse	......	140,952	112,208	150,129	165,851	20,499	7,324
Toyonaka	19,819	46,093	43,765	86,203	97,973	28,349	3,041
Suita		65,810	64,803	78,415	84,921	20,452	3,834
Yao	......	......	......	66,698	76,532	18,986	3,513
Itami	15,264	33,579	48,921	56,348	61,225	21,490	2,622
Moriguchi	13,984	41,904	43,263	58,053	65,324	5,429	10,693
Ikeda	......	34,923	40,248	45,177	48,558	21,994	2,054
Ibaraki	......	......	......	34,820	43,820	20,545	1,695
Neyagawa	......	......	......	30,077	32,340	20,700	1,453
Total	2,887,244	4,068,627	1,755,072	3,055,008	3,587,672	466,567	6,548
Towns and villages:							
Nakakawachi Co.	104,492	137,011	172,196	183,155	188,838	91,601	1,999
Kitakawachi Co.	45,547	55,690	94,094	73,635	79,657	40,007	1,846
Minamikawachi Co.	31,998	40,312	51,094	56,163	58,835	32,373	1,735
Mishima Co.	19,260	28,766	45,505	51,407	48,307	74,048	694
Toyono Co.	13,660	22,344	28,285	36,329	41,558	40,070	907
Semboku Co.	6,680	11,199	15,824	20,814	28,278	3,840	5,420
Total	221,637	295,322	406,998	421,503	445,473	281,939	1,495
Total	3,108,881	4,363,949	2,162,070	3,476,511	4,033,145	748,506	4,645
Population ratio:							
Cities	92.9	93.2	81.2	87.8	89.0	62.3	
Towns and villages	7.1	6.8	18.8	12.2	11.0	37.7	

average density of population for the whole area was 4,645, that of the cities was 6,548 and of the county districts, 1,495. For the whole country the average density is 219; for all cities it is 1,574, and for all county districts, 149. These figures illustrate that the area under review is much more thickly populated than the average for the country as a whole. What is worthy of note is the fact that there is a fairly large discrepancy between the figures at night and in the daytime. The night population of large cities is usually much smaller than by day because thousands of commuters throng in from the suburbs. This pendulum movement was more evident in the city of Osaka after the war as a consequence of the devastation of other cities. At the time of the Manchurian and China struggles, the nation was attempting to strengthen its defensive power, and industrial activity was centered in large cities. The population of Osaka and its satellite cities increased from 100 (index) in 1933 to 141 (index) in 1940, whereas that of the county districts rose only to 133 in the corresponding period. However, during the five years from 1940 to 1945, the city population considerably decreased while that of county districts increased. The dispersion of essential industries and the redistribution of population to relieve overcrowded Osaka, in line with the national defense program, partly accounted for this tendency. The largest direct cause, however, of the exit from Osaka was the continual, large-scale air raids which began on March 14, 1945. In all, the number of people affected was 1,130,000. As a result, the population of cities went down to 43 (index) in 1945 as compared with 100 (index) in 1940. In the city of Osaka itself, the population index decreased to 49 while that of the county increased to 138 in the same period. After 1945 (the year the war ended), the population of both cities and county districts grew, but that of Osaka was less in 1953 than it had been in 1933. Taking 1940 as a basis of 100, the population in 1950 showed 88 for cities (72 for the city of Osaka) and 151 for county districts. The pendulum movement of nighttime and daytime population between cities and county districts had always existed but it was made violent by the devastation of the cities. Judging from a survey made in 1951, half a million people move to Osaka from the suburbs daily, when its population is one-fourth larger than it is at night. Expenditures are administered on the basis of daytime population and revenues on the basis of the population at night. Here arises the problem of adjusting city finance to the finance of surrounding counties.

TABLE 36

TOTAL EXPENDITURES AND PER CAPITA EXPENDITURES OF 67 MUNICIPALITIES, 1933, 1940, 1945, 1950, AND 1953

	Total Expenditure (In thousand yen)					*Per Capita Expenditure (In yen)*				
	1933	*1940*	*1945*	*1950*	*1953*	*1933*	*1940*	*1945*	*1950*	*1953*
Cities:										
Osaka	139,351	200,876	216,072	21,647,544	37,373,431	52	61	196	11,066	15,964
Amagasaki	972	3,884	19,460	1,307,745	2,972,579	17	14	127	4,682	8,766
Sakai	4,391	4,116	15,322	1,472,658	2,231,213	35	23	92	6,991	9,659
Fuse	......	2,276	5,738	1,083,001	1,188,068	..	16	51	7,213	7,163
Toyonaka	337	738	2,985	729,675	1,129,991	17	16	68	8,464	11,534
Suita	......	852	2,480	513,422	952,293	..	12	38	6,547	11,213
Yao	......	......	......	280,897	642,046	..	..	..	4,211	8,389
Itami	288	308	1,559	246,101	602,021	19	9	32	4,367	9,832
Moriguchi	215	502	1,995	252,428	549,330	15	12	46	3,709	8,407
Ikeda	......	677	1,649	240,208	621,814	..	19	40	5,317	12,805
Ibaraki	......	......	......	146,824	524,163	..	..	..	4,217	11,961
Neyagawa	......	......	......	65,540	345,562	..	..	13	2,179	10,685
Total	145,554	214,229	267,260	27,983,043	49,132,511	50	52	152	9,160	13,695
Towns and villages:										
Nakakawachi Co.	744	1,334	3,534	392,094	726,760	7	9	20	2,140	3,848
Kitakawachi Co.	389	565	1,592	178,961	476,169	8	10	17	2,430	5,977
Minamikawachi Co.	249	413	967	110,435	225,186	7	10	18	1,967	3,827
Mishima Co.	187	285	842	123,925	180,242	9	9	18	2,410	3,731
Toyono Co.	114	321	595	137,371	209,815	8	14	21	3,781	5,048
Semboku Co.	178	230	374	50,136	115,207	26	20	23	2,408	4,074
Total	1,861	3,148	7,904	992,922	1,933,379	8	8	19	2,356	4,340
Total	147,415	217,377	275,164	28,975,965	51,065,890	47	50	127	8,335	12,662

ANALYSIS OF LOCAL EXPENDITURES

As stated above, according to a survey made in 1950, whereas the areal ratio between cities and county districts is 62.3 percent and 37.7 percent, that of population is 87.8 percent and 12.2 percent, pronouncedly in favor of cities. The ratio in city finance is proportionately even greater—an overwhelming 96.0 percent, with the balance of 4.0 percent for county districts. The city of Osaka is a typical example: it has 25 percent of the area, 56 percent of the population, and 76 percent of the finance. The total expenditures and per capita expenditure in the fiscal years of 1933, 1940, 1945, 1950, and 1953 are shown in Table 36.

The per capita expenditure for 1953 is 4,340 yen for county districts and 13,695 yen for cities, about 3.2 times that of county districts. The saying that expenditure increases in proportion or some times even in geometrical ratio with increases of population may perhaps be exaggerated, but as shown in the table, the per capita expenditure of cities with large populations is larger than those of county sections, and among cities, the city of Osaka, with the largest population, spends more money per capita than other cities with small populations. There are of course some exceptions such as Toyonaka and Ikeda, cities in which per capita expenditure is exceptionally large in proportion to their population, but this is due to extra outlays of temporary nature such as the erection of new hospitals, etc. In a community of scanty population, life is so simple that most of the living activities can be taken care of individually, but as population increases, people have to depend more on social intercourse, and the per capita expenditure naturally increases. The following table is prepared to show the relationship between the total expenditure and per capita expenditure by index for 1940, 1945, 1950 and 1953, taking 1933 as a basis of 100.

The figure for 1933 can be taken as that for a normal prewar year. The local finance and tax system was newly established in 1940. After the period of World War II, and the postwar era, a novel local tax system was adopted in 1950 at the recommendation of the Shoup Commission. In comparing the index figures for 1933 with those for 1953, the increase of the total expenditure as well as the per capita expenditure for county districts is larger than those for cities, namely 542 times for county districts and only 273 times for cities in per capita expenditure. That for the city of Osaka is smaller than any of other surrounding cities except Sakai. These data show that the relation between cities and

TABLE 37

INDEX OF TOTAL EXPENDITURE AND PER CAPITA EXPENDITURE OF 67 MUNICIPALITIES

	Index of Total Expenditure					*Index of Per Capita Expenditure*				
	1933	*1940*	*1945*	*1950*	*1953*	*1933*	*1940*	*1945*	*1950*	*1953*
Cities:										
Osaka	100	144	155	15,535	26,820	100	117	377	21,281	30,700
Amagasaki	100	400	2,002	134,130	305,820	100	82	747	27,541	51,565
Sakai	100	94	349	35,538	50,815	100	66	263	19,974	27,597
Fuse										
Toyonaka	100	219	885	216,521	335,309	100	94	401	49,788	67,847
Suita										
Yao										
Itami	100	107	542	85,451	209,035	100	47	168	22,984	51,747
Moriguchi	100	233	926	117,408	255,502	100	80	306	24,727	56,060
Ikeda										
Ibaraki										
Neyagawa										
Total	100	147	184	19,225	33,755	100	106	304	18,252	27,390
Towns and villages:										
Nakakawachi Co.	100	179	475	52,701	97,683	100	128	286	30,571	54,971
Kitakawachi Co.	100	145	409	46,005	122,408	100	125	212	30,375	74,712
Minamikawachi Co.	100	165	388	44,351	90,436	100	143	257	28,100	54,671
Mishima Co.	100	152	450	66,270	96,386	100	101	200	26,778	41,455
Toyono Co.	100	281	521	120,501	184,048	100	175	262	47,262	63,100
Semboku Co.	100	129	210	28,166	64,723	100	77	88	9,261	15,669
Total	100	169	425	53,354	103,889	100	100	238	29,450	54,250
Total	100	148	186	19,656	34,641					

TABLE 38

CLASSIFIED EXPENDITURES OF 67 MUNICIPALITIES, FISCAL 1953

(In thousand yen)

	Assembly	*Office*	*Police and Fire Service*	*Public Works*	*Education*	*Public Welfare and Labor*	*Public Health*	*Encouragement of Industry and Commerce*	*Local Debt Service*	*Total Expenditures*
Cities:										
Osaka	94,118	4,870,240	3,894,112	4,710,324	3,078,555	3,826,468	1,317,157	299,626	1,008,966	36,733,650
Total excluding Osaka	170,821	1,370,451	1,187,195	834,496	1,160,813	1,231,217	389,640	319,329	323,321	11,029,652
Amagasaki	37,258	474,805	400,481	349,405	236,790	370,433	82,397	115,188	113,002	2,972,579
Sakai	11,810	209,226	193,861	154,766	280,953	325,886	59,496	83,007	93,357	1,948,247
Fuse	16,491	100,544	144,526	53,527	116,140	136,092	62,756	32,379	23,511	1,145,359
Toyonaka	17,781	86,081	84,787	31,695	122,242	50,334	31,282	12,238	18,923	1,022,221
Suita	16,116	84,309	72,306	70,486	51,979	63,902	44,061	8,800	19,028	827,501
Yao	14,093	94,355	52,857	15,508	82,435	54,889	10,605	13,329	5,185	701,732
Itami	13,591	116,129	65,284	37,496	99,339	85,070	34,381	18,909	12,925	602,021
Moriguchi	11,935	49,488	45,936	22,226	61,805	42,871	40,926	4,673	10,300	552,809
Ikeda	11,620	57,900	47,820	47,680	48,580	51,680	7,770	9,170	10,600	541,978
Ibaraki	12,194	61,639	33,413	36,192	38,716	36,387	4,701	13,566	11,514	399,598
Neyagawa	7,932	35,975	45,930	15,515	21,834	13,673	11,265	8,070	4,976	315,607
Total	264,939	6,240,691	5,081,307	5,554,820	4,239,368	5,057,685	1,706,797	618,955	1,332,287	47,763,302
Towns and villages:										
Nakakawachi Co.	20,846	197,079	53,234	48,390	181,928	50,022	48,838	33,582	18,916	726,760
Kitakawachi Co.	9,595	95,925	16,433	53,571	80,868	51,052	8,543	30,134	8,883	476,169
Minamikawachi Co.	4,260	53,794	16,283	23,137	45,743	52,450	21,676	18,995	3,748	225,186
Mishima Co.	5,298	48,212	8,906	13,296	39,930	27,953	5,455	16,444	4,886	180,242
Toyono Co.	7,601	41,408	13,607	26,442	37,769	3,003	7,807	8,285	4,033	209,815
Semboku Co.	2,329	29,967	2,242	15,598	22,996	9,701	3,480	2,487	2,408	115,207
Total	49,929	466,388	110,705	180,434	409,234	194,181	95,799	109,927	42,874	1,933,379
Total	314,868	6,707,079	5,192,012	5,725,254	4,648,602	5,251,866	1,802,596	728,882	1,375,161	49,696,681

county districts in respect of both total expenditure, and per capita expenditure in 1953 was more equalized than in 1933. Several reasons can be offered for this tendency. In the first place, the inhabitants and facilities of cities were removed to rural districts to escape air raids and they have not completely been restored. Secondly, the county people were inspired to manage local functions themselves; functions primarily conducted by the city of Osaka are now being performed by its satellite cities. Of course, this equilibrium presupposes assurance of local revenue sources.

A striking difference appears in the public enterprise expenditures of Osaka, its satellite cities, and county districts. By public enterprise, we mean water works and transportation; the cost of these are wholly borne by municipalities. Public enterprise expenditures for fiscal 1950 occupy a proportion as large as one-quarter of the total expenditure of Osaka, one-ninth of that of other cities, and one twenty-third of county districts, showing the characteristic in expenditures of Osaka.

Expenditures other than public enterprise expenditures can be classified into nine groups: assembly; office; police and fire service; public works; education; public welfare and labor; public health; encouragement of industry, commerce, and agriculture; and local debts service. The detailed figures of these expenses for fiscal 1953 are given in Table 38.

The percentages of each group in relation to the total expenditure of Osaka, its satellite cities, and county districts are shown in Table 39 and Chart 6.

TABLE 39

PERCENTAGES OF CLASSIFIED EXPENDITURES OF 67 MUNICIPALITIES, FISCAL 1953

	Osaka	*Other Cities*	*Towns and Villages*	*67 Municipalities*
Assembly	0.3	1.5	2.6	0.6
Office	13.3	12.4	24.1	13.5
Police and fire service	10.6	10.8	5.7	10.4
Public works	12.8	7.6	9.3	11.5
Education	8.4	10.5	21.2	9.4
Public welfare and labor	10.4	11.2	10.0	10.6
Public health	8.2	3.5	5.0	3.6
Encouragement of industry and commerce	0.8	2.9	5.7	1.5
Expense for local debt service	2.7	2.9	2.2	2.8
Total	100.0	100.0	100.0	100.0

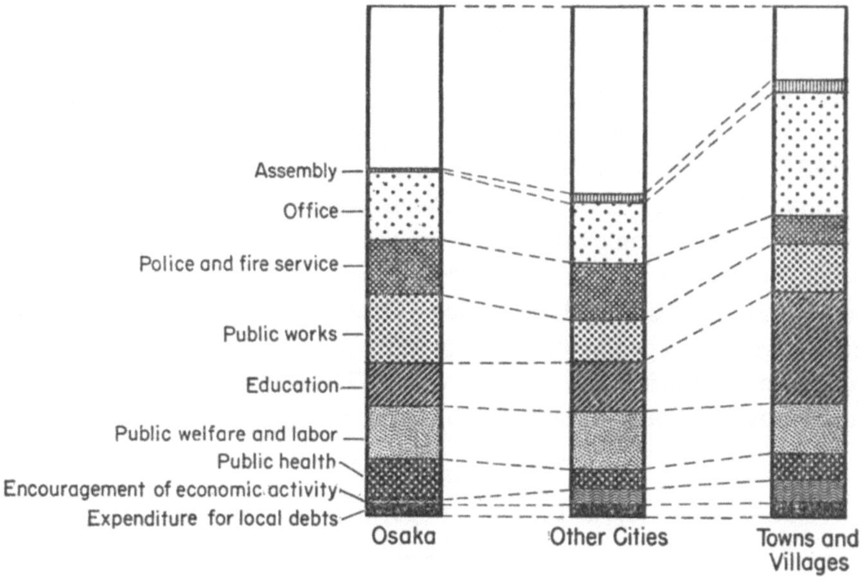

CHART 6

CLASSIFIED EXPENDITURES OF 67 MUNICIPALITIES, 1953

Excluding public enterprise and miscellaneous expenditures not included in the list, the rank in percentage of total expenditure is as follows:

Expenditures	*Osaka*	*Other Cities*	*Towns and Villages*
Office	1	1	1
Public works	2	5	4
Police and fire service	3	3	5
Public welfare and labor	4	2	3
Education	5	4	2
Public health	6	6	7
Local debt service	7	7	9
Encouragement of industry commerce and agriculture	8	8	6
Assembly	9	9	8

Apart from public enterprises, the major items of local expenditures are represented by office, police and fire service, public welfare and labor, public works, and education. It is obvious that while the items naturally vary in accordance with the different needs of local bodies, all cities, towns, and villages spend the largest sums for office maintenance.

ANALYSIS OF LOCAL REVENUES

Local revenues consist of four parts. The first includes the inhabitant's tax, property tax, electricity and gas tax, and other independent taxes all of which are collected within the administrative area. The second is a local finance equalization grant allocated from the national treasury. The grant is necessary because some important revenues in the corporation tax, income tax, and others are national taxes and inaccessible to local authorities and also because the financial inequality among cities, towns, and villages must be adjusted. In the third place, there are dues and charges (except for public enterprises), subsidies from national and prefectural treasuries, and local bonds. The fourth source of local revenue and by no means an unimportant one, is from public enterprises.

TABLE 40

CLASSIFIED REVENUES OF 67 MUNICIPALITIES, FISCAL 1953

(In thousand yen)

	Independent Taxes	*Local Finance Equalization Grant*	*Subsidies and Grants from Treasury and Prefecture*	*Local Loan*	*Total*
Cities:					
Osaka	12,834,060	236,711	4,862,998	2,762,300	36,733,650
Total excluding Osaka	4,031,193	476,351	1,041,136	651,220	10,129,238
Amagasaki	1,426,588	1,000	334,839	164,500	2,232,698
Sakai	710,000	150,654	259,040	141,100	1,948,247
Fuse	391,722	118,359	100,692	66,500	1,145,359
Toyonaka	322,052	2,145	48,845	42,500	1,022,221
Suita	263,864	21,610	53,804	53,200	827,501
Yao	187,494	66,922	56,904	30,100	701,732
Itami	247,951	1,500	54,864	54,000	441,488
Moriguchi	144,594	49,945	35,251	35,000	552,809
Ikeda	173,432	9,104	48,680	31,900	541,978
Ibaraki	100,089	21,320	31,845	23,420	399,598
Neyagawa	63,407	33,792	16,372	9,000	315,607
Total	16,865,253	713,062	5,904,134	3,413,520	46,862,888
Towns and villages:					
Nakakawachi Co.	372,278	124,014	68,890	77,900	792,641
Kitakawachi Co.	194,234	36,203	58,253	50,290	463,318
Minamikawachi Co.	88,998	37,135	36,852	18,300	252,642
Mishima Co.	96,014	16,625	29,773	23,570	185,702
Toyono Co.	119,447	4,000	18,369	14,600	227,362
Semboku Co.	77,848	6,298	11,445	5,300	117,698
Total	948,819	224,275	223,582	189,960	2,039,363
Total	17,814,072	937,337	6,127,716	3,603,480	48,902,251

According to the figures for fiscal 1950 the size of revenue from public enterprises varies widely among cities, towns, and villages. It represents as much as 25.6 percent of the total revenue of Osaka, but only 12.2 percent in other cities and a negligible 3.8 percent in county districts. Table 40 shows the amount of revenue from items other than public enterprises. The items are taxes, local finance equalization grants, subsidies and grants from treasury and prefectures, and local loans. The figures are of fiscal 1953.

Table 41 and Chart 7 show the percentage of each of the four items in Table 40 to the total revenue of Osaka, its satellite cities, and county districts.

TABLE 41

PERCENTAGES OF CLASSIFIED REVENUES OF 67 MUNICIPALITIES, FISCAL 1953

	Osaka	*Other Cities*	*Towns and Villages*	*67 Municipalities*
Independent taxes	34.9	39.8	46.5	36.4
Local finance equalization grants	0.6	4.7	11.0	1.9
Subsidies and grants from treasury and prefecture	13.2	10.3	11.0	12.6
Local loans	7.5	6.4	9.3	7.4
Total	100.0	100.0	100.0	100.0

As shown in Table 41, apart from public enterprise revenues, the bulk of revenues of Osaka comes from independent taxes (34.9 percent) and subsidy and grants from treasury and prefecture (13.2 percent), and local loans (7.5 percent); the local equalization grant is almost negligible (0.6 percent). The revenue composition of other cities is not greatly different—independent taxes, 39.8 percent, subsidy and grants, 10.3 percent—except for the local equalization fund which is 4.7 percent, much larger than that of Osaka. In the revenues of county districts, the percentage of the equalization grant is high, 11.0 percent, and other revenues are also fairly high—independent taxes, 46.5 percent, and subsidy and grants, 11.0 percent.

Up to World War II, the financial status of Osaka had been distinguished from any other satellite cities but, as stated before, the finance of county districts has since been inflated much faster than that of Osaka, through reinforcement of local revenue sources. The dispersion of inhabitants and facilities of Osaka to satellite cities or near-by county districts during the war strengthened local finance by increasing revenues

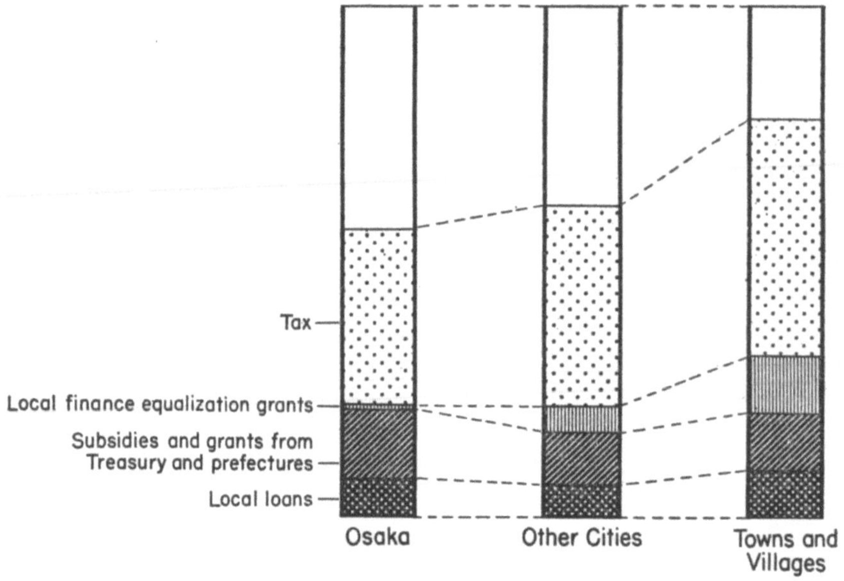

CHART 7

CLASSIFIED REVENUES OF 67 MUNICIPALITIES, 1953

from independent taxes (inhabitant's tax, property tax, and electricity and gas tax). The local finance equalization grant which assured the standard financial requirement has a similar effect.

CONCLUSION

So far the financial analysis has been made on the fiscal figures of 1933, 1940, 1945, 1950, and 1953 of the city of Osaka and sixty-seven surrounding cities, towns and villages. These five fiscal years were chosen because each had a particular significance, except 1933, which was considered as a normal year to be used as a basis of comparison. Although the area is small, it is the center of economic activity in Japan. As surveyed in 1950, its population is 4.2 percent of the total and its financial scale is equivalent to 9.3 percent of the total finance of all cities, towns, and villages of the entire country. It is a model area to study the changes brought about by World War II in local finance.

1. Average per capita expenditure of the large city is greater than that of middle and small size cities, and that of county districts is least. This is to be expected because of the varied intensity of social problems in these local units, and has been statistically proved.

2. The great prewar financial gap between the large, middle-sized, and small cities and county districts has been gradually narrowed. This was a natural consequence of the dispersion of economic power to rural districts to escape war disaster and of the administrative policy of buttressing local finance by the local finance equalization grant.

3. There is an infinite variety in the local units. Take the scale of population, for instance. According to the 1950 census, the city of Osaka has 1,956,136 residents as against 2,165 of Futajima village of Kita-Kawachigun. The majority of inhabitants in some towns and villages were born there, and are descended from generations of farmers born in the same locality.

Index

Bei Fragen zur Produktsicherheit wenden Sie sich bitte an:
If you have any questions regarding product safety,
please contact:

Walter de Gruyter GmbH
Genthiner Straße 13
10785 Berlin
productsafety@degruyterbrill.com